LIFE IN THE SHADOWS

A JOURNEY OVERCOMING PTSD, ADDICTION AND CHILDHOOD SEXUAL ABUSE

NANCY LEGERE

First Edition

Cover design: www.fiverr.com/germancreative/
Layout and typesetting: Cheeky Kea Printworks, www.ckprintworks.com
Editor: Marlene Oulton, www.MarleneOulton.com

This book is not intended as a substitute for the medical advice of physicians. The reader should regularly consult a physician in matters relating to his/her health and particularly with respect to any symptoms that may require diagnosis or medical attention.

TABLE OF CONTENTS

FOREWORD

When I first met Nancy in May 2016, she was looking for help in getting ready for her upcoming discovery hearing which was scheduled for a few months later. She was 30+ years sober and no longer struggling with thoughts of suicide. Her loving partner of 20 years was already a solid, supportive, and unwavering presence in her life. She had already been successfully self-employed for numerous years and found a sense of stability in her work. All of these things continue to be true today. But to her it felt like something was missing. In her words that first meeting, "Even though I have no idea what "it" would look or feel like, I want to start experiencing more in life." Her hope was that speaking her truth and holding the man who raped her accountable for his actions, would help her claim this possibility of "something more." But to do that, she would first need to find the words to clearly express what she had lived through – to find a way to give voice to what had previously been unspeakable. This book emerged spontaneously from that process.

I think it's safe to say that nothing since that first meeting has gone according to plan, or according to schedule. Repeated delays of her court proceedings stretched months into years. This unpredictability caused heightened anxiety, and all of its related challenges, to become a near constant reality for her. We paused, and then continued again, numerous times. We allowed our focus to gently shift and evolve as different aspects of her past and present experience emerged for attention. It has not been easy. Yet through it all, Nancy has remained committed to seeing this process through to completion. I believe there have been a few key things that have helped this to be possible: the inclusion of complementary therapies; her connection with nature; and her love for her partner.

Psychotherapy in general and trauma therapy in particular, has been actively evolving in acknowledgement of the mind-body connection and the body's vital role in mental wellness. A few important leaders in this integrative approach include Dr. Bessel van der Kolk, (*The Body Keeps The Score*), Pat Ogden, PhD, (founder of Sensorimotor Psychotherapy), Peter Levine, PhD, (*In An Unspoken Voice*), Dr. Gabor Maté, (*When The Body Says No*), Stephen Porges, PhD, (*The Polyvagal Theory*), and Joan Borysenko, PhD, (*Minding the Body, Mending the Mind*). This is by no means an exhaustive list; however, it offers a helpful place to start for anyone wanting to better understand the potential benefits of what used to be considered "alternative" therapies as a complement to their current mental health supports. The inclusion of body and energy-based therapies was crucial in our work together, as we needed a comprehensive approach to calming her heightened stress response in particular, and regulating her nervous system in general, especially when talking was simply not an option. This included Emotional Freedom Techniques (EFT – acupressure tapping), breath work, binaural stimulation (sound therapy derived from Eye Movement Desensitization and Reprocessing (EMDR), meditation, and gentle physical movement. It also included working with a massage therapist, an acupuncturist, and several different energy workers. Overall, Nancy's (eventual) willingness to try these complementary therapies meant that they were available to support her health and healing beyond the limits of what traditional psychotherapy could offer.

One of the strategies for stress reduction used consistently throughout our time together was purposeful time connecting with nature, even if just watching the birds in her yard through a closed window during cold winter months. Nancy and her partner had already created a beautiful oasis in their backyard, so there was always something beautiful, interesting, or entertaining to observe. Her deep appreciation of nature was already there. We just expanded on this intentionally to incorporate a practice in mindfulness – pausing to notice what is, as it is, becoming more fully present in the process. An unexpected outcome of this practice has been a burgeoning friendship with one of the visitors to her yard: a female pheasant named Charlotte. Not only will Charlotte tap at her patio door to say hello, she'll even eat some seeds right out of Nancy's hand while letting her stroke her head. They feel safe with each other, calm and content – a beautiful gift of connection which has brought its own healing energy into her life. She fully realizes that these moments of contentment are possible in unexpected ways, and after years of feeling so much darkness, offers her encouragement to keep going.

It has been well documented that a feeling of meaningful connection, of feeling loved unconditionally, and of having our needs acknowledged and met in a responsive manner, can protect us from the potential psychological harm of traumatic experiences. It can also help us to heal from these same experiences. The absence of this kind of support can make healing much more complicated. Throughout Nancy's story, we see examples of how this was true for her – as it would be for anyone in her same situation. We witness the added layer of trauma from not being believed, her struggle to feel worthy of love and support, and her exposure to future abuse as a result. We hear her acknowledge, even if just in hindsight, the importance of people stepping into her life to offer her support, especially in moments when it felt like there was no hope left, and how crucial this was in her recovery. And we feel the transformative power of fully embracing the loving presence of another into her life, even when she was still struggling with feelings of shame and unworthiness. More than anything else, it has been Nancy's love for her partner and desire to have the best life possible together that has kept her anchored in a sense of purpose when it otherwise would have been tempting to walk away.

Through her writing, Nancy offers us a rare and courageous glimpse into all of this and more. We get a glimpse into the devastating and complex nature of traumatic injury from childhood sexual abuse and all of its associated symptoms. We witness first-hand how our survival instincts can help us live through the unlivable and then cope with the aftermath. We are reminded of the power of meaningful connection in bringing healing, purpose and possibility into our lives. And perhaps, most importantly, we are shown by vivid example that it is possible to heal from trauma.

Tina Antle, MSW, RSW, nd,
Karuna Counselling

ACKNOWLEDGEMENTS

I dedicate this book to all who have been my angels during this journey. My life partner, Denise, played a tremendous role in shaping who I am today. She believes in me much more than I could ever believe in myself and has always loved me unconditionally. So many people from across this beautiful country have held me up and walked with me when I was unable to, and have played such an integral role in how I was able to write this book.

Heartfelt thanks to Tina for writing the Forward and to Elisabeth, Connie and Dawn for their contributions to the Perspectives section providing valuable insights on the topics discussed in this book.

You often hear people say, "There's always a light at the end of the tunnel." Mine was more like a candle and at times it would flicker and almost burn out. And just as I was about to give up hope, someone would be put on my path and offer me a new candle. Some even had several wicks which would carry me through long journeys to get to the end of the tunnel, while others were short, small candles that required more intense help. I've had numerous people go out of their way to help me even when I didn't want it.

Some got me sober while others made sure I stayed that way. Some took me in even when they didn't know me, and some became amazing lifelong friends who never judged me, while others passed in the night, but left a mark. I will be forever grateful for all who have touched my life including a great team of professionals whom I've had the privilege to learn and work with throughout the last thirty plus years so that I could reclaim my life.

A friend recently compared my journey to that of a character called "Scrat" from the movie *Ice Age*. His sole purpose in life is to bury an elusive acorn which always, always triggers calamitous events. That could very well sum up my journey – forever trying to bury my secrets and everything that came along with them.

In this book I share with you my journey overcoming Post-traumatic stress disorder (PTSD), addiction, and childhood sexual abuse.

CHAPTER 1
LOSS OF INNOCENCE

I was the second born of three girls in a family of humble beginnings. My parents were hard workers in a time when both parents working out of the home was somewhat rare. We had nannies while growing up, but for us, that was the norm.

I will try to piece together a cohesive picture of what I remember life was like for me, but unfortunately some of my memories tend to be a bit scattered. I also know that my memories may not always be what the people around me remember. We all see things differently and what registers in our mind depends on how it affects us at that moment. I will trust my memories as well as incorporate other information shared with me while writing this book.

I remember very little of my childhood prior to the age of seven and some of the information that I have of those years has been passed on to me by my siblings and parents. My father often spoke to me about the time I spent in the hospital as a child at around the age of eighteen months and how they were unable to visit because they didn't have a car and the hospital was an hour away. He still chokes up when he talks about getting a phone call in the middle of the night from the hospital telling them that I might not make it through the night. Despite all that, I survived and made it back home. To this day, I don't know what the medical issue was that had made me so sick and by now it isn't really that important.

The main thing to note here is that my behavior had changed by the time I returned home. From what I was told I was now afraid of the dark which would make sense since hospitals are truly never dark even at night and I had become accustomed to sleeping in rooms with several night lights. I can also see why that bond I had with my parents would have been damaged, and that as a child all I could possibly understand was that I was left behind. I am not in any way blaming my parents, rather simply stating the circumstances of my early childhood and how this could have been perceived by a child.

In November, 2016, I had the opportunity to attend a workshop by Dr. Gabor Mate on Trauma and Healing, and he used the above example almost word for word to explain what he calls "the attachment disorder." I quickly found myself wondering if maybe this is what made me susceptible to being victimized. Yes, I still have times were I think I need a reason for why things happened so that I can make sense of it all. What I also know about myself is that I can quickly turn this into something that was broken in me and therefore that would have been the reason why all these things happened. I have since decided not to explore this any further for now.

By all accounts and from information I've been able to gather, my childhood was normal. We were regular kids doing what kids did in those days. We took swimming classes and played outside in the yard. The year before entering school I would have plastic surgery done. My parents were concerned that I would feel different and be teased because my ears were not fully attached to my head and stuck out through my hair. A local doctor agreed to do it at no charge. Even back then this would have been deemed a cosmetic procedure and basically would have had a cost attached to it. My parents would not have been able to afford it at the time.

I've seen photos of myself and I am glad they chose to have that done. Having somewhat protruding ears would have certainly added a level of difficulty to my life growing up. I remember being in the hospital for that surgery. At times I can still see the layout of the room I was in and the corner crib assigned to me. I was at least four years old at the time, if not older, and I'm sure being restricted to a crib would have also had an impact on me. Plus it must have registered somewhere in my brain that I'd done something wrong as my parents had again left me behind.

There is another thing I remember from that hospital stay. I was either walking or running back to my room when I bumped into the doctor. I remember him as a very big man. I was carrying wax crayons and a coloring book and some of the crayons broke during this mishap. I was a bit upset over that accident as I loved coloring. I'm not sure how long after this incident happened, but this doctor actually replaced my waxed crayons with really large ones that wouldn't break. That memory has always stayed with me in a good way.

I experienced a drastic change in what was to become my new normal at the tender age of seven and from that day on it would affect every aspect of my life for many years to come. That night would change my life forever.

It was not unusual or foreign to us to be babysat while growing up so that my parents could get away when they wanted to go somewhere. One such evening in October 1972 was to be no different. My parents were heading out to the local hospital to spend some time with my older sister. I don't recall the reason why she was hospitalized. We always had the neighbor's daughters as babysitters, but this evening neither one was available and my parents agreed to have one of the neighbor's sons babysit for a few hours. He was fourteen and old enough to watch over me and my younger sister.

I was on the floor watching TV which was not unusual for me. I'm not sure what we were watching. My younger sister was already in bed. He was stretched out on the sofa and asked if I would lay with him. I'm sure the fact that attention was paid to me was likely the reason I did as he asked. One on one attention doesn't happen in a family with three young children very often and I certainly had no indication or reason to believe that I shouldn't do it.

It didn't take very long for me to feel in my gut that something was very wrong. He slipped his hand down my PJ's and my body reacted to it. He got aroused in a matter of seconds and what was a pleasant feeling turned to fear. He became aggressive and even the look on his face changed. He threatened to hurt my younger sister if I didn't do as he said. To this day I'm not sure where the overwhelming sense to protect my younger sister came from, but I didn't dare go against his instructions.

I can still see him sitting at the edge of the sofa with his pants unzipped holding his penis. He put one hand around my throat and forced me to perform oral sex on him. It was really hard for me to breathe and I felt like I was choking. I remember being terrified and was just too young to understand what was happening. It seemed like it lasted forever.

The next thing I remember is being naked on the living room rug. He was on top of me, raping me. It was physically excruciatingly painful. Again the weight of his body made it difficult for me to breathe. This feeling of never having enough air is still with me today. I recall after awhile feeling like I was frozen and staring intensely at one strand of wool of the orange shag rug covering the living room floor. I think being able to do that made it possible for me to emotionally survive what was happening. My body was there, but I no longer was feeling or hearing anything.

I'm not sure how long any of this lasted. My next memory is lying in my bed facing the wall. I just wanted to go to sleep. My thoughts were that this was all a bad dream and it would all be gone when I woke up. I remember needing to use the bathroom, but was too afraid and sore to go. I fell asleep and when I woke up the next morning I had wet the bed.

CHAPTER 2
GUILT AND SHAME

It still amazes me to this day to think that somehow between the time I went to bed and when I woke up the next morning, I was already convinced that what had happened must have been my fault. I had to have done something very wrong to have caused him to rape me. That sense of guilt and shame stayed with me for many years and it still rears its ugly head at times. Maybe it's how I was able to justify what happened in order for it to make some sort of sense to me. I very quickly became embarrassed when I noticed I had wet the bed, and at the only thing I could think of is my parents would be upset with me for having soiled my sheets.

Not knowing what to do, I got out of bed, went outside, and sat on a swing that we had in the backyard until my mom came to get me. The mind is a very powerful thing and will protect us when trauma is that great. It would be forty-two years later, almost to the day, before I would come to realize it was my mother who came to get me. For all those years I assumed it was a nanny. In October, 2014, I found out while visiting my parents that we no longer had nannies when I was seven. This realization played a big part in writing this book which I will explore further in later chapters.

I don't remember anything ever being said about the bed wetting or being outside on the swing in my soiled pj's. As usual, I was dressed and sent off to school as if nothing ever had happened. That was very confusing for me and it reinforced the feeling that I must have done something wrong or that I was in real trouble.

In later weeks, I started to develop massive headaches, to the point where I would throw up. These seemed to occur frequently and were alarming enough for my parents to consult with our family doctor. I was eventually sent to a hospital about three hours away from our home and given a brain scan. Back then those tests were quite different from the scans of today. At that time, a "scan" meant sticking lots of wires to my head. I remember the fear I felt thinking that they would know what I had done.

Now I was surely in trouble. See, I had been keeping this secret for awhile and these wires would tell them what that secret was all about. I know that was just the imagination of a child, yet I remember it vividly seeming to be so true to me. This was not a good experience for me and I can definitely say it added to the trauma I'd already suffered.

I'm not sure what the results were from those tests, but I assume the headaches were diagnosed as juvenile migraines since no tumors or abnormalities were found. Now when I see a seven or eight-year-old child, I can only imagine how frightening my world must have been during that time frame. Being able to somehow disassociate myself from the happenings made it possible for me to survive. I learned how to shut my brain off and pretend the rape never happened. I don't remember if I had nightmares at the time, but I do remember having them when I was twelve or thirteen. The kind of nightmares where you wake up and you can still hear the screaming in your head and your heart is beating a hundred miles per hour. They feel very real and it's almost impossible to fall asleep afterwards. Getting a full night sleep is still very much a luxury for me.

I learned from all my years of therapy that it is not uncommon for a child who has been sexually abused to be more susceptible to further victimization. That would prove to be true for me as I was re-victimized on a regular basis from the ages of ten to thirteen by a different man. It was not violent or painful, and although it never included intercourse or rape, having to repeatedly perform oral sex and touching him left me feeling sick and dirty. There had to be something very wrong with me because it kept happening. Obviously the fact that he was sixteen when it started while I was only ten, and at the end when it finally ceased I was thirteen to his nineteen, certainly changed the dynamics. He always had all the power. It wasn't fun for me or something I liked or wanted.

These feelings of shame and guilt were intensified by the years of continual abuse. It also reinforced in me the feelings of being damaged and dirty. We were brought up in the Catholic faith which certainly didn't help alleviate any of these feelings. In my youth, a strict code of faith was taught in school and I had to take catechism lessons at the church. Today I'm not a religious person and do not associate with any manmade religion, yet I think of myself as somewhat spiritual. Somewhere along the way my siblings and I were taught to pray, so I began to pray every night that God would come to get me and take me away from this earth. I started asking for this event to happen when I was around eleven years old. I'm not sure I understood what suicide meant at the time, but I knew that I didn't want to be who I was. Thus began my battle with suicidal thoughts which would last well into my forties, becoming progressively worse as the years rolled by.

I'm not sure how many years I prayed to die before I accepted the fact that even God didn't want me. I believed I was certainly not worthy of anyone's attention and I started to hate myself around the age of eleven. That belief never wavered as time wore on.

I would certainly not be a person one would call vain. Even today looking in a mirror is uncomfortable for me and for years I avoided doing so. I think this was a bit of a shock to Denise when she first moved in with me. The only mirror was in the bathroom and she needs a last chance mirror on just about every wall to check her hair and makeup before leaving the house. I say this in a good way and love this about her. She takes great pride in her appearance so we now have mirrors everywhere in our home.

It's the strangest thing. I believe I actually trained my mind to see only specific things. For example, while fixing my hair in the morning, I truly have to make a conscious effort to actually see my face in the mirror, otherwise I will only see the hair. Again, the mind is a very powerful thing and will allow you to do whatever is needed to survive.

Both guilt and shame became driving forces in my life and would be the hardest feelings for me to deal with. At times I would compensate by trying to be the perfect student and loose myself in school projects if challenged enough. On the other hand, it would also fuel my addictions as well as my self-destructive behaviors.

CHAPTER 3

GROWING UP

I don't remember forming close relationships with people or my family. I always felt like I was different and on the outside looking in. I thought if they got to know me they surely wouldn't like me. Growing up was very lonely for me and I often found solace in my intellect. I was smart and this made it hard for me to remain challenged in grade school. I would often get bored and become distracted in class. I remember being sent to stand outside the classroom on a few occasions in the second grade for misbehaving. Not sure if these were for short or long periods, but everything seems long to an eight year old. The teacher would come and get me when she felt it was time for me to rejoin the class.

The teacher realized I was more advanced than the curriculum and suggested at one point to have me pushed ahead to grade three. My parents chose not to do that for fear I would struggle making friends in a different age group. My mother had experienced that problem in her own life having graduated from college at a very young age and felt she never fit in with her classmates. She wanted to shelter me from that so I remained in grade two.

We moved to a new house before I started fourth grade. I remember my sisters making friends quickly and having sleepovers, but I can't seem to recall doing that. I don't remember who I hung around with at the time or who my good friends might have been. I remember going fishing with some of the boys and playing basketball, hockey, and softball, but no one I would consider a real friend. I seemed to hang around with the guys more than girls. I wasn't much of a girly girl and I was bigger and stronger than the guys I spent time with, so maybe it felt somewhat safer to spend time with them. An added bonus was that surely the boys wouldn't be able to figure me out as easily as some of the girls might have done.

I was also very good in sports as this allowed me to release a lot of my pent up anger. I was very fortunate to have a grade four teacher who took the time to make me feel special. She also made me feel smart and that I mattered by often rewarding me for scoring well on assignments. There was something about her. She made that classroom a safe place for me and I loved going to school. I remember being good at writing and it was something I enjoyed along with reading. Unfortunately, my love affair with school was to end after that grade year finished. I have in the last several years found a love of writing again which encouraged me to write this book.

Sometimes things come full circle. I reached out to this teacher last year. It was important for me to let her know she had made a real difference in my life. Technology today makes it pretty easy to find people and I was able to send her a letter. She responded in writing that she was very pleased to know she had made a difference in my life and at the same time saddened to discover that I had suffered in silence for all those years. Her reply, although not expected, was heartfelt and her words of encouragement will stay with me on this journey.

Most of my report cards were recently found in my parents' basement when my dad was going through some old boxes. I have to laugh to think that only mine seemed to have survived all the family moves over the years and were found just as I started writing this book. I was a very intelligent kid and maintained high marks until high school. My average marks were in the nineties until the seventh grade, and started slipping to mid-eighties in the eighth and ninth grades. By that time I had started drinking on a more regular basis which clearly affected me by the time I got into High School.

The seventh grade is where I started to struggle more to fit in. Once again I was at a new school as the previous one only went up to the sixth grade. Some of the students needed to make sure you knew it was their territory. I would spend a bit of time in the vice principal's office. I don't recall being reprimanded or punished; she would just bring me in and try to talk to me a bit. I wasn't a very big talker so I just listened. She also was a person who made me feel safe. I was never afraid or uncomfortable with her; it was like she understood what I was going through yet I never spoke about anything.

I would have the opportunity to see her again some twenty plus years later and she remembered me like it was yesterday. When I first ran into her, I found myself on the receiving end of a big hug. She was genuinely happy to see me and appeared to have fond memories of those days. Funny how she never forgot me. I think she knew I struggled back then which is why she took the time to talk to me and try to help.

As time passed, I eventually became the bully. By being aggressive, it kept people away from me. That followed me to a subsequent school where I attended the eighth and ninth grades. I don't remember specific events during those two years, but knowing my character and the amount of anger and hurt I was carrying, it wouldn't have taken much for me to lash out at people around me, especially if they were vulnerable. It was a trait in myself I hated the most, yet I used it as a shield to keep people from trying to get to know me.

I began having more problems at school and was visiting the principal's office on a regular basis for bullying or being a distraction in class. I was good at sports, but had now lost the ability to control my emotions which cost me my spot on the badminton team. I still remember the pain of that happening to this day. We were training for a tournament that included teams from different Atlantic Provinces. It was to be the first year of these games and I didn't make it. I was disappointed and angry. However, I did make the softball team the following year and attended the second year of "Jeux de l'Acadie" (Acadian Games) in 1980. They are still going strong thirty nine years later.

Being a good little Catholic girl also meant going to confession at church. I'm not sure I really knew what that meant except that you told the priest all the bad things you did and you'd be forgiven. It was 1977 or 1978 and times were changing back then. You no longer had to go into a confessional box: you just lined up and waited for your turn to kneel at the front of the church and whisper your sins in the priest's ear. That would be the last time I would ever go to confession, and more than likely one of the last times I ever entered a church other than to attend a wedding, funeral, or baptism. I thought church would be a safe place for me. It turned out to be anything but that.

My turn came and I nervously whispered to the priest that I must have done something really bad for these things to happen to me, but I didn't know what I had done. I was telling him about the sexual abuse and that it was happening again. He looked at me and in a loud and angry voice said that liars like me ended up going to hell. He kept on speaking, but that's all I heard — that I was going to hell. Those words would stay with me for a very long time. To say I was embarrassed would certainly be an understatement. It was as if the priest added another layer of shame on to my already growing pile. I walked out of that church and went directly home.

The next week when it came time to go to church I made my way there, went inside to get the weekly bulletin to show my parents that I had gone, and walked out. I spent the hour I was supposed to be inside the building behind it at the recreation centre smoking cigarettes and sitting on one of the swings. This was to become my new way of attending church. Given the stories of sexual abuse that have come out over the years relating to the Catholic Church may explain the priest's reaction and beliefs. However, his reaction intensified the feelings of guilt and shame to a level that became almost unbearable for me.

CHAPTER 4

REBELLIOUS YEARS

Into my teenage years I found what would become my savior and allow me to get through the days (and nights) without committing suicide. Its name was alcohol and I fell in love with it. I don't recall the exact date I started to drink, but I do remember my grandmother once giving me burnt toast and black tea to help ease my morning after hangover which was probably the result of a Christmas Eve family party or some sort of family gathering. My grandmother passed away in November 1978, so that meant I was thirteen at the time and drinking was already a part of my life.

I grew up in a generation where weekend house parties were very common modes of entertainment. Our household, like most at that time, had a very generous bar and I realized very early that it didn't take much of whatever was in those bottles to make me feel anything other than who I really was. I felt okay when I drank; it gave me a sense of normalcy. I also started smoking cigarettes during this timeline as well. I don't think I got drunk regularly as my soul purpose of doing it was to feel numb when the pain became too much to handle. That feeling of blessed numbness would become my norm for a very long time.

You could often find me somewhere off by myself listening to music. I grew up with all the great country singers such as Tammy Wynette, Loretta Lynn, Crystal Gayle, Carol Baker, Dolly Parton, Kenny Rogers, etc., as well as bands like Creedence Clearwater Revival and other types of music. I was able to get lost in melodies and found it very soothing. It was like I was in their world and not living in mine.

I did odd little jobs to earn a few dollars such as cleaning my dad's office on the weekend. I would dust, empty the garbage cans, sweep the floors, and clean the bathroom. I would also scrub the floors if needed. One day while dusting, I came across a letter on his desk. I wasn't a nosy kid by any means, but I saw my name on it so I read it. My parents had joined this group called Marriage Encounters as a way to improve their relationship and part of the process was writing letters to each other. I remember from this letter that my mother was saying she found it difficult to allow herself to love and bond with me because of almost losing me when I was a child.

As a teenager I interpreted that to mean she simply didn't love me and who could blame her. In my mind I was a horrible person. The priest had confirmed that fact when he told me I would go to hell for lying that last time I went to confession. He'd given me the belief that he was in direct contact with God, and since God had never answered my prayers, that was proof enough for me. I certainly understand today that wasn't what she meant at all. And now that I know some of my mother's life story I can understand why she needed to protect herself from having to deal with losing another child. The doctors and nurses kept telling them I wouldn't make it and I can only imagine how difficult that must have been for her as a mother. I'm certain that at some point anyone in similar circumstances would just shut down to minimize the pain. I know that's what I did.

Around the age of fourteen, with my parents written permission, I managed to get a job in the kitchen of the local hospital. My main job was to work on the food line preparing the trays of food for the patients, and then do dishes or prepare sandwiches for another meal. It provided me with spending money to buy cigarettes and alcohol. For some reason, I never had a problem obtaining alcohol and it wasn't illegal to sell cigarettes to minors in those days. It was not unusual for me to show up for work on Saturday mornings hungover as hell. Everyone at work just made fun of it, including myself. Nobody seemed to think it was a big deal.

On one particular Saturday morning, I was sent to get the bread and butter for the breakfast line and while I was in the cooler someone shut the door behind me. That would be the first time I remember having a feeling of being trapped and not able to breathe. I panicked and started to bang on the door not knowing there was a way to open the doors from the inside. I don't think I was there very long before someone let me out, but by that time total panic had already consumed me. That's where I remember having my first flashback to the attack. Plus I can still see the smirk on the person's face that had shut the door on me. She thought it was funny and never realized that what she did would impact my life for a very long time and not in a good way. I became even more distrustful of people after that day.

By the age of fifteen, alcohol was now very much a part of my daily life. My parents were aware that I was somewhat out of control, but figured I would outgrow it as most teenagers do. Alcoholism was something that was not discussed nor recognized in teens thirty plus years ago. Up until then I had maintained good grades in school and never had to work hard to get them either, so by all accounts things still appeared normal. I was quickly becoming a very angry teenager and I don't think that my parents were able to do very much at the time to stop me from doing whatever I wanted to do. Grounding me didn't work as I would simply climb out my bedroom window and be back before they even knew I was gone.

With regards to school, I remember there were only two teachers who truly made a positive impact on my life. The first I've already mentioned, and then there was my eighth grade teacher. She was unlike any other teacher we had at the time. She often would stay late along with her husband and supervise my friends and I in order to allow us to use the gym and play any sport we wanted. She was also very caring and I could feel that. I had even considered talking to her during that year as I was struggling and knew I was in trouble. Yet I felt stupid and was also afraid she wouldn't believe me anyway. Obviously the priest's reaction left a much deeper and long lasting effect than I had initially thought.

This was the first year that we were taught the very basics of sex in school. Even with all I had been through, I knew very little about it and would certainly never ask for fear of being made fun of so I tortured myself for an entire year. During one of the classes I heard that you got pregnant by having intercourse and that's all the information we were given. I was convinced that because of the rape seven years prior I must surely be pregnant, not knowing that it was impossible. I was so naive about the subject of sex. I spent that entire school year fearing I was pregnant and everyone would now know what I was damaged and dirty. The internet was not a luxury available to us in the late seventies, so to research or Google anything did not yet exist. Plus I surely wasn't about to be seen looking for information on these topics at the library. I wouldn't have even known where to look and certainly wouldn't ask the librarian for help.

The eighth grade was also the start of gym classes. Because of the small change rooms which contained only two or three fully enclosed bathroom stalls, getting ready for gym meant undressing in front of my classmates. I was already so uncomfortable with my body that I always waited for a stall to be available to change clothes. I was sure that if anyone saw me partially clothed, something about my body would give my secret away. Like it was stamped on me somewhere that I was damaged goods.

Something changed in the summer between eighth and ninth grade. I didn't care about anything anymore. I began to drink more and was now very much in trouble with alcohol. My life was spiraling out of control. It seemed that I was always in some kind of trouble. Unfortunately alcohol put me in situations that no teenager should ever be in and I grew angrier and angrier. I was kicked off the badminton team because my temper had become an issue. I didn't care much about anything anymore and started to think more and more about suicide. My grades started to drop and one teacher noticed as I ended up in her class again in the ninth grade. There was nothing she could do to help me. By this time, I was emotionally unreachable and travelling a path of self-destruction.

Alcohol created situations that only reinforced what I thought of myself at the time. For me it was official: I was a freak and I worked very hard to never allow anyone into my world for fear they would figure that out. Dating was not something I even considered a possibility. Just the thought of someone touching me made me sick and no amount of alcohol seemed to be able to change that. All I knew about sex was what I had experienced to date; therefore I never knew that those occurrences were certainly not the norm. I was never physically attracted to either a male or female, but I think even back then people assumed I was gay just because I didn't have a boyfriend and was very much a tomboy.

Flashbacks and nightmares became a part of my daily life which I managed to control with alcohol. As these episodes increased, so did the drinking. This past year Facebook has given me the opportunity to reconnect with some of the people that I knew back then, most of whom I have not spoken to or seen in over thirty years. It was interesting to have the opportunity to ask them a few questions about their perceptions of me back then. I didn't think anyone had noticed how out of control my drinking had become yet I was told that a few friends had actually confronted me about it. I guess that explains why I just quickly drifted away from them. I didn't want anyone to interfere with my escape route via alcohol and I didn't care anymore. Others found me a bit different, but assumed that I was gay and not comfortable with my sexuality so they didn't pry. I'm not sure I even knew what being gay meant back then.

By the time I made my way to high school I had found myself another job. I was now working forty-four hours per week and going to school as my hours were every day after school until 9:00 pm and every weekend from 9:00 am to 9:00 pm. I was earning good money for a teenager which only fuelled my addiction. I worked as a gas bar attendant at a service station which just happened to be next door to a liquor store. To me I had found heaven. I made friends with the local drunks that hung out around the gas station therefore obtaining alcohol was never a problem. All I wanted to do at the time was drink. Oblivion was far better than my reality and as destructive as alcohol was, it kept me alive.

The rite of passage at sixteen was to get one's driver's licence. We were fortunate to be a two car household and my parents made one of those available to my sister and me. They trusted and assumed that we would be responsible drivers. To be honest, my sister was probably better at driving than I was. I remember driving the car into a ditch after a night of drinking and partying at the age of seventeen. I had offered to drive someone home and didn't quite make it to their house. Since she lived just around the corner from where the accident happened, she went into her house and called a tow truck for me. I still remember sitting in the car, drinking and singing along with the radio when the tow truck arrived to get the vehicle out of the ditch.

The tow truck driver was someone I knew. He let out a big sigh of relief when he saw who was driving the car. I saw a big tear roll down his cheek as he explained he had just finished hauling away a vehicle at the scene of an accident where several young girls had died after their car was hit by a drunk driver. I think that sobered me up for the moment. It wasn't the thought of me dying, but the thought that I could cause someone else to die that was sobering. Unfortunately as teenagers, we feel indestructible and think that those things won't happen to us anyway. That memory quickly faded and I would repeatedly drive while drinking. It wouldn't be the last time he would come to my rescue.

CHAPTER 5

SPIRALLING OUT OF CONTROL

Eventually I went to work for a retail store as a sales clerk. My high school years are a bit foggy with only bits and pieces of events which at times make it hard for me to know exactly when things happened. This job would eventually play a very important part in the beginning of my journey into recovery, which I will touch on more in subsequent chapters.

At one point I began dating a guy, but I can't recall how or where we met. I was trying hard to fit in and I was going to achieve that by having a boyfriend. It would end badly after a night of heavy drinking. All I remember is being in his car and him becoming aggressive. He felt that since I didn't want to have sexual intercourse then I should at least perform oral sex on him. I started to panic, he got angry. The evening ended with me having a cracked rib and a fat lip.

I was about twenty miles from home and walked most of the night until my friend's father, a local tow truck driver, picked me up and drove me home. Yes, it was the same tow truck driver that had previously towed me out of the ditch on a few occasions. I would always remember what he did for me. He never asked what happened and I didn't feel like he was judging. I was so ashamed and embarrassed that I had allowed this to happen. I never saw that so called "boyfriend" again and never talked about that evening.

Dating was not something I would ever be successful at even when I became sober. I did try, but mainly because I thought it would make me fit in and I desperately wanted acceptance. I wanted to be what I perceived to be normal which in my mind wasn't anything like me.

I was often heard saying that I needed to live it up since I would more than likely never see my nineteenth birthday. People around me thought that was funny, but I truly believed that and making it to nineteen was a far stretch for me. I was just biding my time as I was already dead inside. By the time I was sixteen, all I wanted to do was drink and not have a care in the world. I wanted to be permanently numb. I knew I would never have a significant other. I was convinced that I was unlovable and certainly not worthy of it anyway. I also knew I would never have children.

High school was not pleasant for me. I drank as often as I could and suffered severe blackouts. I didn't fit in and felt like a freak. Post-traumatic stress disorder (PTSD) was very much a part of my life at the time with flashbacks, depression, and nightmares occurring regularly, but it would be many years before I would even know what that was or be properly diagnosed.

I managed to hang on to my job as it was something I enjoyed. Most of my co-workers seemed to like me and I felt like I was good at something. There were times when I showed up for work pretty hung over and more than likely still drunk, but I always managed to make it through my shift. For some reason, that was important to me.

Graduating from high school was no longer something I strived for and I wanted to drop out. I had always managed to keep most of my marks just above the exemption bar for writing exams, but by twelfth grade I was barely getting by and had no interest in school at all. The drinking eventually earned me a suspension at the end of eleventh grade, but I didn't care. I was found passed out on the floor in one of the school's bathrooms before 10:00 am on the very last day of regular classes. Exam time was to begin the following week. I remember very little of that day.

Punishment was a suspension of three days at the beginning of the following school year. It also meant I lost all my exemptions for the current year and would be required to write all the exams. Somehow I got passing marks on all my classes and the suspension didn't hold. I had registered at a different school for the following year as I had chosen to attend the English high school which fell under a different school district. Until this point I had always attended the French school in my hometown. Nothing felt like it had any real consequences anymore.

I switched schools for my twelfth grade just to have easier access to alcohol. I often spoke of quitting school and was more than likely talking about it while on break at work. The assistant manager's wife somehow heard about it and befriended me. She offered to tutor me through that last year and felt it was important for me to graduate. I, on the other hand, didn't think it would make much of a difference. I was very depressed and often thought of suicide. The alcohol, which was slowly killing me, was the only thing that could make me feel better or at least I thought it did. I'm not really sure how we became friends and I can't recall if she ever tutored me, but I did graduate at the end of that school year. I remember very little of that year or how I got through it alive.

A friend agreed to come with me as my prom date but we didn't stay very long as he wasn't feeling very well. Just long enough to take a few photos and make it look good. I found all of it extremely uncomfortable. First of all, me wearing a dress was a rarity along with having my picture taken. These were things I usually avoided like the plague. You still won't find a dress anywhere in my closet. I like to look good yet I'm far from being a girly girl. Jeans, jogging pants, and sweatshirts were my usual attire during that period.

I didn't have any plans after graduation since I had already lived longer than I had expected. I picked up a few more shifts at work, but wasn't really going anywhere in that job. Shortly after graduation, the assistant manager was transferred to PEI to manage his own store and it meant that his wife would also be leaving. I must have grown on them because they offered to take me with them. I don't think they realized the extent of my addiction. I was told years later that her husband said to her "If someone doesn't take her out of this town she will die." His gut feeling was right and his intuition would set in motion the beginning of my journey into recovery.

I moved shortly after they got settled in their new home. I was boarding with them while working at the store. I was excited to discover that the legal age to obtain alcohol in PEI was eighteen. Finally I would legally be able to drink and nobody could say anything about it. I find it ironic that just as I was legally able to drink, I began a path to sobriety. However my happiness would be short lived. I found myself drinking more and pretty much all the time. The blackouts grew worse and at times I would leave for work in the morning and make a small stop at the liquor store on my way just to replenish my "stash" for the day, only to return home three days later not having showed up at work and not knowing where I had been. To this day, I have no recollection of where or who I might have been with during those times. My drinking had spiralled out of control and reached a level where it was just a matter of time before it would kill me.

We lived in an upstairs two bedroom apartment of a duplex which meant I was sharing this space with two other adults and a baby. It certainly made for tight quarters and the baby and I shared the same room. I don't remember very much else and I can't recall how long I stayed with them. I've had the opportunity to see that lady two or three times over the last ten years, but have not had the opportunity to ask what she remembers. Our lives have taken us on different paths and we have very little in common now except for having shared that space during that period of my life.

CHAPTER 6
BEGINNING OF RECOVERY

Early one evening there was a knock at the door. I was home alone and drinking which, come to think of it, was not a common occurrence for me to be alone in the apartment. I would eventually come to realize that this random visit had been on purpose. The person at the door was a sister of our downstairs neighbor. I can't recall what she said that made me let her in, but I did. Unbeknownst to me, she was a recovering alcoholic and as the evening progressed, I remember her asking me about my drinking. I'm sure I wasn't the most welcoming person at that very moment and got quite angry at the thought that they would set me up. I don't remember anything else from that evening. I know we met again, not sure how or where, but I recall sitting in an Alcoholic Anonymous meeting thinking what the hell did I get myself into. I remember feeling really stupid and couldn't seem to follow much of what was going on.

I couldn't tell you how many times I was taken to meetings or if I managed to stay sober for any length of time during this period. At this point I didn't think anything or anyone could help me. I was spiritually, physically, and mentally broken and had given up. I don't know who took me there, but I also recall going to a treatment center. I'm not sure if it was just for a meeting or if it was to have me admitted as a patient. In my drunken stupor I thought it was a psychiatric institution and decided that I'd rather be dead than be there. So I climbed out a bathroom window and ran like hell. I don't know where I went, but I was told that I was missing for a few days and then just reappeared like nothing had happened.

I remember two ladies in particular trying to help me get sober while I was living in PEI. The one who first came to see me in the apartment and a second one who I can still recall today, but have never had the opportunity to see again after leaving the Island. They both played a big part in helping me eventually find sobriety and my introduction to Alcoholics Anonymous. The first lady let me live at her home for a while and she recently told me she remembers me coming in one day after falling off the wagon. Again, I was sick from drinking and thinking she would be really mad at me. All she said to me was "While you're down there on your knees (with my head in the toilet bowl), could you please say a prayer for me?" I can imagine that went over well with me, but today I can find the irony in her statement.

Although brief, my time on the Island felt like it was a lifetime. I don't remember exactly when I moved back to my hometown, but I do know I was there by my nineteenth birthday. At this point I'd been in and out of Alcoholics Anonymous for a while. I would get small periods of sobriety, but was never able to maintain it. I did have a sober nineteenth birthday and again that would be short lived. I made sure, however, to get my liquor ID just for identification purposes, or at least that's what I told everyone. I never expected to stay sober.

My father gave me a job as a receptionist/bookkeeper in his accounting business for which I'm now grateful as I'm not so sure anyone else would have hired me at that time. I had no experience in that field but seemed to catch on fairly quickly. That would be the stepping stone to what would become a very successful career for me as I would make my way in the accounting industry. Sometimes family members will be the ones to give you a break and help you get back on your feet when no one else will.

June 24, 1984, would become my official sober date and has remained unchanged to this day. That was a little more than two months after my nineteenth birthday. It would be the last time I would have a drink. Just before that date, I had joined a softball team thinking the drinking would not be an issue for me. Well, I was wrong. Some of us had decided to go camping for the weekend at a local campground and we also had some kind of a ball tournament. After a full day of playing softball, we all agreed to meet at a local pub for food and a few drinks. Of course, I'd tagged along because after all, I had to eat.

I was awakened by a security guard at the campground as I was lying in the middle of a field after failing to find my tent. By this time I also couldn't find my car. I had probably wandered away looking for the bathroom and gotten lost. At least I still knew my name and he escorted me back to my tent where my car had been parked. I have no recollection of driving my car that evening yet I left with it that morning. That thought stayed with me for a long time. I was always so sure I could handle a few drinks, but this time was different. This blackout actually scared me. Maybe something was starting to sink in during the few weeks of sobriety I had managed to get previously from attending meetings.

Again, I returned to Alcoholics Anonymous with my head hanging low. I had failed again. I was ashamed and embarrassed and vowed this time would be different. This time I was going to make it work. An Alcoholics Anonymous member and his wife offered me room and board as I was currently without a place to live. I'm not sure why they wanted to help, but I accepted. It was going to be a fresh start for me. The member took me under his wing, and drove me to meetings everywhere and every night. I kept hearing them say 90 meetings in 90 days so I was certainly on the right track. I surrounded myself with sober people and stayed sober. The first few months in Alcoholics Anonymous are pretty foggy and it would be a while before I would be comfortable there.

Alcoholics Anonymous became my life. I stayed busy by going to meetings and eventually got involved at the group and area level. By this time my dad had sold his business and eventually moved on to manage his manufacturing company full time, but I stayed working for the new company for a while. I even attempted to take some courses in accounting as I needed to stay busy. You see, now that I was sober and no longer had anything to anesthetize the PTSD symptoms; I was starting to remember things. I didn't know anything about PTSD at the time or how it presented itself in someone's life. All I knew was I would get flashes of memories that occurred out of the blue. I slept as little as possible due to constant nightmares. I had figured out that if I didn't allow myself to fall into a deep sleep I wouldn't have nightmares, so most nights I drifted off watching programs on TV. Somehow the noise from the TV offered a feeling of safety. It was if the voices reassured my mind that someone else was there with me.

June 24, 1985 eventually rolled around. That day marked my first three hundred and sixty-five days of non-interrupted sobriety. I had finally achieved something that was positive. I had always felt like such a disappointment to my family for being what I was convinced was such a screw up, and finally now I could show them I was doing better. The Alcoholics Anonymous group that I belonged to celebrated such anniversaries at an open monthly meeting where they would get you a cake and you could invite non-members to celebrate with you. I invited my parents. I suppose even as an adult I still needed them to see that I could be someone other than a screw up. They didn't make it to my celebration and all I remember feeling was that again I wasn't good enough. I'm sure it wasn't meant that way, but that's how I perceived it. I would never celebrate another anniversary. It just became unimportant, like it wasn't a big deal anyway. I've been sober now for over thirty-four years and never celebrated my sobriety anniversary.

In Alcoholics Anonymous they suggested I find what they call a sponsor, someone that I could talk to and who could help me stay sober, so I chose a person sometime after my 1st year anniversary. We spent pretty much of the next ten years going all over the place for meetings and conferences. Since I wasn't a talker, I learned to listen really well. And she loved to talk, we made a good team. You can truly learn a lot by listening, but I also spent way too much time living in my head. Nobody really knew how much I was struggling and I couldn't seem to talk about it. I was convinced that I had deserved everything that had happened to me so far in my short life, so the shame and embarrassment made it impossible for me to let anyone into my world.

Some people would call some of the things I did to survive extreme measures, but for me it's what was needed at the time. I often had problems eating after I sobered up. More times than not the texture of food triggered the PTSD making it hard for me to swallow to the point where I would vomit. I decided that my only solution was to have all of my top teeth pulled out and replaced with a full set of dentures. This provided a barrier to the palate which affected the taste and texture of food making it possible for me to eat. It was a practical solution that required no explanation other than I had bad teeth and they needed to be removed.

My first two years in Alcoholics Anonymous were basically uneventful. I worked all day and ran to meetings every night. It became a safe haven for me and at the time made me feel like I was ok, that I belonged somewhere. I would even be asked to speak occasionally at meetings, sharing a little bit of what it was like when I drank and how I got sober. At the time it seemed important to have people see me and tell me how well I was doing, but that nagging little voice in the back of my head was always there. I was always on my guard not to let anyone know very much about me. They certainly wouldn't like what they saw; at least that's what I felt to be true. I hated who I was and surely they would too if they *really* knew me.

Those feelings of shame and guilt were always there. They were deeply embedded in my being. At times Alcoholics Anonymous certainly wasn't the best place for me. As in any other organization, you have people from all different walks of life and some are sicker than others. It was not unusual to be hit on by men old enough to be my father and some more my grandfather's age. Given my background with sexual abuse, these incidents were very problematic for me and often left me feeling dirty. Even three showers a day couldn't wash those feelings away.

Once I got sober I noticed I was having a hard time touching my own skin. This meant having to wear full length PJ's and shirts with sleeves long enough that my arm couldn't touch the sides of my body. I actually would breakout in welts if I placed my hand directly on my arm or leg. It was if I had developed some sort of allergy. That is still an issue I deal with today and have to wear at least 3/4 sleeves and nothing shorter than capri's no matter what the temperature is outside. I also noticed my inability to handle raw meat. Watching me in the kitchen can at times be very entertaining especially if I'm cooking meat or trying to cut raw meat. I still gag if I accidently touch raw meat and it sends shivers up and down my spine.

One thing I noticed is that you learn very quickly to live with these things and adapt the best way you know how at the time. I've never really given it much thought nor tried to change it since it wasn't really a big issue for me until this past year. One of the techniques known to help with the PTSD is called Emotional Freedom Therapy (EFT, colloquially known as "tapping") which applies pressure with your fingers to certain points on the body. This has caused me some anxiety mainly because I would consciously need to touch my skin. A second option has been acupuncture where the needles do it for you. We are still experimenting with both modalities, but I am getting a bit better with being able to touch my skin.

I managed to put together a fair sized music collection throughout the years as I'd always loved that mode of entertainment. Amazingly enough, my records and cassettes made it through the worst of my addiction and were mostly intact when I sobered up. Yes, this was prior to CD's, DVD's, USB's and streaming services. I decided to put all that memorabilia to good use and setup a small, part-time DJ business for a year or so. I did a few weddings, Christmas and New Year's Eve parties. I enjoyed the fact that it kept me busy doing something I enjoyed as I still found music very soothing.

Organizing the music as well as setting up all the equipment helped me feel like I was good at something. I know music can be very therapeutic for some and I think on some level it was for me as well. I don't listen to it as much anymore except for when I'm in the car or at times while working. It always seems to make me feel good and I'll often find myself singing along.

I've always loved to sing – just not in front of anyone. Actually the only one that has ever heard me sing is my partner, Denise. But don't expect to see me on stage anytime soon. I'm far too shy for that nor is it on my bucket list of things to do. She likes my voice so I often sing to her when we are driving. It's also good therapy for me, especially when the anxiety gets a bit out of control. Singing helps to regulate the breathing and reduces the anxiety which is an added bonus.

CHAPTER 7
DESPAIR

Life as I knew it would come to a crashing halt after a weekend away camping in August 1986. I woke up the Monday morning in excruciating pain and standing up or walking was nearly impossible. Eventually I made my way to the doctor only to be told it was more than likely just a back sprain and that I should feel better in a week. This dragged on for quite a while. I was no longer physically able to work and attempted on numerous occasions to get the doctor to fill in the proper papers to get Employment Insurance and my short term disability from work. It would take eight months for him to finally get that done. For eight months I was told it was all in my head and that nothing was wrong, yet I could barely stand up and walking was agonizing.

So I found myself not able to do much of anything except lay on the sofa and watch TV or get lost in my thoughts. Getting lost in my thoughts was certainly not a luxury I could afford at the time and I became very depressed. The doctor hospitalized me for probably a week to see if putting weights attached to my feet and stretching my back would help ease the pain. It was a quicker way to be to get into physiotherapy since I had already been admitted as a patient. At the same time he sent a psychiatrist to see me. That did not go over very well. She spent a total of maybe an hour with me. I had grown very angry and depressed because of the back injury and now I had this person standing there asking what I perceived to be stupid questions. I already didn't trust people in general and by this time doctors were not very high on my list of "safe" people. Nothing ever came of this meeting and I never saw her again. I had the opportunity several years later to look at my medical records to find out that she had diagnosed me as having a Borderline Personality Disorder. Really. She determined that in less than a one hour meeting knowing nothing of my background or life. I also learned in later years that people with PTSD are often misdiagnosed as having this disorder.

November would begin the fourth month with no improvement in my back. By this time I had more muscle relaxants that didn't work and pain killers that I wouldn't take for fear of getting addicted. I grew increasingly more depressed since all I could do was lay there and think about my life and how screwed up it was. After all, I'd been sober for more than two years yet still felt like I would never make be successful at anything. Why would someone like me even deserve to be happy? I was doomed to fail. I thought of suicide every day wishing I could muster up the courage to do it. As much as that nasty little voice was always in the background, so was another little voice that every once in a while would say, " Just hang in there a little longer."

I made another visit to my family doctor. At least this time he finally ordered a myelogram which is an x-ray taken once dye is injected in your system to see where the abnormalities are. While in the doctor's office, his nurse asked if I was having suicidal thoughts and I told her I did. It's not like I had anything to lose. I was asked if I would go see someone in the emergency department. This person turned out to be a psychiatrist, actually the husband of the one I had seen a few months earlier. I really didn't care anymore who I saw as I just wanted it all to end. I was broken in every possible way. I'm not sure how long I was there, but when I decided I'd had enough and got up to leave he simply said that if I didn't agree to treatment right then and there he would have to call security and the police, and I would not make it to the front doors. I was now deemed a threat to myself and possibly others.

I've had the opportunity this year to have access to my medical records relating to this stay and once again without any background or insight on my life, I was once again diagnosed as having a Borderline Personality Disorder after stating that the prior assessment (made by his wife) was accurate. I will elaborate a bit more on this in later chapters.

Trying to explain what was going through my mind at that time is pretty much impossible. I couldn't believe that I was going to be admitted to a psych ward. How low could I go? It couldn't possibly get any worse, right? I thought of calling his bluff and heading for the door, but I just didn't have it in me to fight anymore. I surrendered, gave up. I remember very little of my two week stay, yet I was not medicated while there. I did have to call my parents so someone could bring me some extra clothing. My dad came to see me. I'm sure this must have been more than uncomfortable for him and certainly very surprising. I had gotten very good at not letting anyone see how much I was struggling so this news came as a shock to my parents.

I still get a chuckle when I recall that day my dad came to the hospital. They were trying hard to figure out why I was there and just what had brought me to this place. All I remember hearing is my dad saying something along the lines of "You know if it's because you're gay we'll love you anyway. We're okay with that." Well, at least now they had a plausible explanation. I didn't confirm or deny anything and I had certainly never given my sexual orientation a thought, but I could understand why they would think that. I was just glad they had an answer that seemed satisfactory to them. That way I didn't have to try and come up with one. I wasn't gay. I'm not sure I even knew what that meant. I was never physically attracted to either male or female which made me basically asexual.

I returned home like nothing happened and I don't remember discussing my hospital stay or anyone asking about it. It would be another six months before I would return to work and in the meantime I tried to get to as many AA meetings as I could despite the pain. I finally saw a back specialist only to be told I was obese and should really try to lose at least twenty-five pounds. He was old and shaky and reeked of alcohol, yet I was the one not worthy of compassion and a little caring. He looked at my test results, but no one ever bothered to tell me what the issue was. Again I was left thinking that all this pain might really be all in my head.

In late March or early April of 1987, I received a call from my family doctor's office; he wanted to see me. Once I arrived he gave me my x-ray results in an envelope and told me to pack clothes for a few days and make my way to Moncton, about two and a half hours from my hometown. I was expected in the Moncton Hospital the next day. I drove myself there and made my way to admission. The lady informed me, "Your surgery is scheduled for tomorrow morning." I'm sure that the shocked and surprised look on my face obviously gave me away. Surgery? She also explained that I would not be able to drive when I left there and I should find someone to come and get my car as the parking fees would be expensive. So now I was totally confused. Obviously my doctor had failed to mention any type of surgery to me.

My older sister lived in Moncton at the time and was attending University. Thankfully she was able to come and get my car. I got settled into my room and waited for the orthopedic surgeon to come and see me. It seemed to take forever, but he finally arrived. He proceeded to tell me that I should be advised that this surgery did have risks and there was always a chance I could be paralyzed. That's all I heard, the word paralyzed. My mind was racing. That morning I had left home thinking I was having a consultation with a specialist and within twelve hours I was now scheduled for surgery with a possible devastating outcome. I was a few days short of my twenty-second birthday and could not comprehend very much of what was happening and was certainly not prepared for it.

An angel visited me that evening and no, I was not delusional. Today I chose to call her an angel because she appeared at the door of my room out of the blue when I so needed somebody. She came in and I recognised her right away. I had been friends with her daughter in school five or six years previously and later they had relocated to Moncton. Just the fact that she took the time to talk to me made me feel like I was worth something. She seemed genuine and very compassionate. It made all the difference in the world. I've never had the opportunity to talk to her again even after living in the same city for about ten years, but I was able to share this story with her daughter asking her to relay it to her mother and thank her so very much for me. I hope the message was passed on as she was certainly a godsend that night.

I remember calling my dad from my hospital room. By now I was really scared, but I tried to hide it. I don't recall much of the conversation, but it must have put my mind at ease enough for me to get some sleep. The next morning I was prepped for surgery, which I'll probably never forget because I had to be awake during the procedure. They gave me a mild tranquilizer along with local anesthetic and proceeded to strap me to the operating table. I was restrained from head to toe to make sure I made no involuntary movements. Of course I started to panic, as once again I knew what it felt like to have no control over my mind and body. I started to sob. The anesthesiologist who was sitting by my head very slowly started to rub my hands which were also strapped to the table. In a very gentle voice she asked if I was feeling any pain. In between the sobs I managed a no. She continued to talk to me and I must have calmed down since the next thing I remember was waking up in my room.

The fact there was a possibility I might never walk again had stayed in my mind and when I became awake enough I decided I would try and see if my legs would hold me up. I really needed to go to the bathroom and asking for a bed pan was way too embarrassing for me. I wasn't able to get the bed rails down so I pulled myself to the end of the bed and just sat there for what seemed like an eternity. Would I be able to stand once my feet hit the floor? I could feel my legs, but that didn't seem to reassure me. Finally I gave myself a little push off the foot board and landed on my feet. What an amazing feeling that was! I would be okay. While climbing back over the footboard after using the bathroom I pulled out my IV. Once I was settled back in I pressed the call button to say my IV must have gotten caught in something while I slept and now needed to be replaced.

A friend came to get me after a short recovery in the hospital. I was one of the first to have a laser surgery to remove a herniated disc which meant all I had was a very small hole in my back where they inserted the laser. Generally you would have at least a twelve inch cut which requires a longer hospital stay. It would be at least six weeks before I would be able to resume work as I wasn't allowed to sit. Eventually life returned to some sort of normalcy. I went back to work at the end of May and resumed my heavy work and meeting schedule.

By this time the depression had eased. I was able to go through life with little emotion. It was like I was able to just turn off the switch. It was a coping mechanism I had mastered as a child. It would bring me to a place where I didn't feel sadness, but I also didn't get to feel happiness or joy. I couldn't pick or chose which emotions I got to experience or shut off. It's all or nothing. It also didn't allow me to form memories the way most people do since emotions are what creates them. It left me like an empty shell of a person, simply going through the motions of living, day in and day out.

CHAPTER 8
EMOTIONAL AND FINANCIAL BANKRUPTCY

Financially, I was finally able to get caught up on my bills once the long term disability issues were resolved after I returned to work. I suppose by now the doctor had to admit that my medical condition wasn't all in my head which was a small consolation after everything I had gone through. At least the short term disability had covered my car loan so I was able to hang onto my car. At that time it was the one thing that made me feel like I had achieved something. It was proof that I had worked hard and had been able to buy myself a car, but it would be short lived as an accident in January 1988 would cause significant damage to my vehicle. Although it was eventually repaired, in my mind it was now like me: no one could see the exterior damage anymore but it was still damaged and broken.

I became more and more involved in the Alcoholics Anonymous program and also with Adult Children of Alcoholics which kept me busy and out of trouble. I met some really awesome people during those years. Today I consider myself very fortunate to have been able to make this journey. For the first time in my life I learned what it was like to have a true friend. I became friends with someone I met through Adult Children who actually liked me for who I really was. Never once did I ever feel any kind of judgement from her no matter what I told her about myself. She was sincere and I felt that. I think it was the first time I ever formed a connection with anyone. We are still amazing friends today and get together for lunch a few times a year. She's played such a big part in helping me to get where I am today.

I would have long stretches where everything seemed under control and I think those were mainly times when emotionally I was just non-existent. I usually preferred to live in my head then in the emotional world. Logic always came easier to me and I became really good at just being who I thought everyone needed and wanted me to be. I projected myself as someone who was full of self-confidence, yet that was the total opposite of who I really was back then. As I mentioned earlier, I hated what I saw when I looked into the mirror so I stopped looking.

I decided that it was time to buy my first home. I found a small mobile home that was ideal for me and settled into it before the end of 1988 or 1989. It remained my home until 1995. I also met someone around that same time who I really liked. We enjoyed spending time together as we both loved to dance. We were on and off as a couple for a few years. It was a very strange relationship as I liked him just as a friend. I had severe issues with intimacy and could not handle having anyone touch me so any other kind of relationship was not something that was possible for me. That feeling of being broken never went away. It didn't matter what I achieved in the material world as success would never fill that hole.

During that time I also experienced severe anxiety attacks which would remain misdiagnosed for several years. They were very similar to asthma attacks since my main symptom would be the feeling that I couldn't catch my breath: the more I panicked, the worse they got. I made many trips to the emergency department for treatment of these asthma attacks. No wonder the inhalers and drug treatments were never really successful. I also came to understand that asthma was very much an emotional disease. I did develop acute asthma, but I no longer suffer from it and haven't required treatment for it in over twenty years.

A good friend referred me to a psychologist who worked with people who had been sexually abused. Even though I hadn't admitted it out loud at that time that it had happened to me, she thought this psychologist might be able to help. I eventually called and made an appointment to see her. We met for the first time December 11, 1990. I was twenty five years old, had been sober a little over six years, and still felt lost. I just couldn't seem to get what could be so wrong with me. The self-hatred I felt could be overwhelming at times along with suicidal thoughts I still experienced.

The flashbacks and nightmares were slowly creeping back into my life, not that they had ever been non-existent, but they'd faded in the past couple of years. Even after taking two showers a day and sometimes three, which I had been doing for several years now, I was never able to wash off the feeling of being dirty. I recently obtained a copy of this psychologist's report which we needed for a civil suit that I will discuss further in the book. I was surprised to find out that indeed she confirmed what I used to say in later years about our visits. I would laugh and say, "I went to see her every second weekend and I never said a word for two years!" I was able to learn some coping strategies and mechanisms from her which would help me function for many years. She was the one that finally diagnosed me with PTSD, but I'm not sure I knew or understood what that was at that time.

Finally, in my third and fourth years of therapy, I was able to share with her in writing a bit more of my story. I slowly managed to find ways of dealing with the PTSD and the symptoms subsided. There were a few people who knew I was seeing a psychologist and one in particular used to travel with me to appointments, especially once my psychologist relocated to Moncton in October 1991. This meant I had a five hour round trip drive for a one hour session. I think the fact that it was out of town offered me some comfort. I didn't want to have to answer any questions as to why I was seeing a psychologist and this offered an extra layer of privacy. There were many trips where my friend would drive us back as I was unable to do so. I would just curl up in the passenger seat and sometimes would manage to fall asleep during the drive home. Other times we would have to pull over to the side of the road because I would get really nauseous and would need to throw up.

We had some good discussions on the way there yet the drive back home would usually be very quiet. I think she grew accustomed to it. I'm not very good at expressing emotions or trying to explain what I'm feeling at the best of times. I was a very logical thinker, and if something made sense to me then I was much better at handling it. Unfortunately, childhood sexual abuse and the damage it leaves behind fuelled by alcohol defy all logic, therefore I often felt confused and lost. Recently I was having a discussion with my current therapist and one word stuck with me long after the session ended. That word was "isolation" and how childhood sexual abuse intensifies this feeling. Looking back at my life I would have to agree. For me isolation was the only way to make sure no one would ever know what had happened, yet at the same time I so longed to be like everyone else.

Everything seemed to be somewhat normal for the next few years. By this time I was almost 28 years old. I had always been very self-conscious of my body and would never show very much of it to anyone. I always wore pants, oversized sweaters, and sweatshirts so the size of my rather ample breasts wouldn't be too obvious, but I would still get comments and stares from people. It became such a problem for me that I opted to have a breast reduction. At the same time, I wanted to erase anything sexual about me so no one would want me. The surgery was very much necessary for my emotional survival and I've never regretted it. I can understand today why I felt I needed it, and yes, these were once again extreme measures.

Life once again returned to some semblance of normalcy. I suppose I could say I was emotionally detached from everything, which allowed me to function in my day to day life. I consider myself an intellectual and combined with my logical sense of reasoning; generally everything for me is either black or white with not much grey in between. I felt like I just existed and figured maybe that was all there was to life so I accepted those feelings at face value. Yet there was always that little annoying voice saying there has to be something else; this can't be it. Not that there was anything wrong with where I was at that time in my life since I wasn't sad or happy or angry. I just wasn't... well, anything.

The one person I had grown really close to got a job in another city and left in 1994. I felt like I had lost my best friend. Over the years we had spent a lot of time together and she got to know more about me than anyone ever had. Given that I wasn't very good at allowing people into my world, I once again felt very isolated and alone even when surrounded by people. I also knew I wanted to leave my hometown and had gone on several job interviews in Nova Scotia and other cities in New Brunswick. I had grown weary with my position as bookkeeper and felt that if I could just up and leave everything behind me and move to another city, life would be better. It would be the summer of 1995 before I would have the opportunity to move.

I had my third car accident in the spring of 1995 while on my way to work. The driver of the other car ran a red light, but since neither one of us had any witnesses the insurance companies deemed it a fifty-fifty split of responsibility. Financially, I would not recover from that accident. I was thirty and still living paycheque to paycheque. I had spent most of my extra money on therapy sessions and Alcoholics Anonymous conferences. The travel alone was more than I could afford, but I needed to be around people. I have absolutely no regrets today as those things kept me alive and functioning.

I'm not sure exactly when I moved to Saint John, possibly May or June of the same year after being offered a job at an accounting firm in that city. My friend who had moved there the previous year and I decided that we would be roommates as a way to cut costs. I had never had a roommate before so that would be a test for me, but it turned out she was away most of the time so I pretty much had the apartment to myself. I had hoped that leaving my hometown would miraculously make me feel better, but it didn't. Things weren't really going as planned. Prior to leaving I had rented my mini home and the tenants turned out to be less than desirable. It ended up that I would never be paid the rent owed to me and they caused a fair amount of damage to my home. I was basically trying to handle paying my rent at the new apartment plus all the expenses for the mini home, including paying the mortgage which the rent that the tenants were supposed to cover. Keep in mind I was still trying to dig myself out of the financial hole the accident and frequent travel had created.

I was getting deeper and deeper in debt and knew that I would have no chance to recover with the salary I was making. I remember calling my father for his advice. I was ashamed and embarrassed that I had failed... again. I needed to tell my parents that I was filing for bankruptcy and that my name would appear in their local paper since the mortgage on the mini home was at a bank in my hometown. My dad was willing to give me a significant amount of money to help me out. He wasn't doing it because he didn't want my name in the paper; he was doing it because he had seen how hard I had worked to get to where I was at that time. I knew I wouldn't recover from this staggering debt and it would simply be putting a band aid on it. I decided not to accept his offer.

September 30th, 1995, at the age of thirty, I declared bankruptcy. I had been sober for eleven years and couldn't believe that after everything I had done to try and better myself I had failed once again. The fact that I now lived in another city eased the impact of the shame a bit, but not by much since the biggest judge of all was the one starring back in the mirror. This was a very lonely time for me. I had cut myself off from everyone mostly because of the shame of having to file for bankruptcy.

I wasn't fitting in very well at my new job. For lack of a better way of putting it, they were really snooty and that type of behavior was not something I was used to experiencing. I used to laugh and say that I was sure one of the partner's slept in his three piece suit as he was that arrogant. I was actually reprimanded for not going to lunch with the staff on Friday's. We weren't paid for our lunch hour nor were they paying for the meal so I didn't see why they were making such a big deal out it. I didn't have a designation nor was I an accounting student, so most people there couldn't be bothered to talk to a technician. I chose not to go, but my absence was frowned upon.

During my time in Saint John, a male friend from my hometown started visiting me on week-ends. We started dating and went to a few events and Alcoholics Anonymous conferences as he was also a fellow member. It was again my attempt at trying to appear normal. I really enjoyed his company, but the fear of the flashbacks never allowed me to be intimate with him. He had recently separated from his wife so this dating scene was all new to him as well. For the most part, he seemed to understand that I had issues. I'm not sure if I ever told him anything about my younger life or if he simply figured out what had happened to me. This whole relationship thing was confusing to me. I was very detached from my emotions and never really knew what it was that I was supposed to feel.

The firm I was working for had offices across Canada, including my hometown. I had worked for them from 1987 to 1989 prior to accepting the new position in 1995. I was asked to transfer to an office back in my hometown in February 1996, so back I went. I was now thirty years old and had nothing to show for working all those years since I had declared bankruptcy five months prior. I moved in with the guy I had been seeing, but that didn't last very long, probably less than a month. We both had a huge amount of baggage that we were bringing into the relationship and neither one of us was ready for it. So I moved into a really nice quiet apartment where I figured I would be for the rest of my life. Once again I felt really defeated and lonely.

By this time I was resigned to the fact that I would never be in a relationship as I felt incapable of handling one, and that I would be alone for the rest of my life. It was somewhat a relief. I would no longer have to try to be normal, and I would just accept I wasn't like everybody else.

CHAPTER 9

FALLING IN LOVE

Being a creature of habit and since I no longer had a car as a result of the bankruptcy, I hung out at a local corner store. It was within walking distance of my apartment, where I would have coffee and read the daily paper. I usually went in wearing dark sunglasses and didn't engage much in conversation. Gossip ran rabid in my small town and I assumed everyone knew by now that I had declared bankruptcy. Denise and I laugh today at how the lady working there used to find me so intimidating until she got to know me. I think the impression of being unapproachable was the impression I wanted to portray to people.

That little corner store had plenty of regulars who came in almost every day to hang out and shoot the breeze with other people. I was introduced to Denise on April 18, 1996, the day I turned thirty-one. In my mind the fact that I had reached that age certainly wasn't anything to brag about, but she wished me a happy birthday just the same. We saw each other there on a regular basis and one day she asked if I would go to the mall with her. I did, even though I'm not much of a shopper, I found out that day that she sure was! I'm the kind of person who will get a newspaper and a coffee, and wait while the other people in the group shop. We certainly were the total opposite of each other, personality wise. She shopped for purses, shoes, clothes and makeup, and always dressed up when going out. I, on the other hand, wore jeans, sweatshirts, sneakers, and no makeup and didn't carry a purse.

The next few months would be a whirlwind of emotions. We fell in love – the one thing I thought would never happen to me. Actually, when I look back at that fateful meeting, I realize that I found my soul mate. I was a bit more guarded with my feelings, but she knew this was the real thing and jumped in with both feet. I couldn't quite understand what was going on, but for the first time I was actually happy and excited about life. I felt alive and scared at the same time. I finally realized that maybe, just maybe, my finding happiness with her meant I was gay. I'm not sure I was overly comfortable with that thought, but it wasn't an issue for her so it became a non-issue for me.

The excitement of a new relationship kept me in the moment, something I had never felt before. Unfortunately, this also triggered trigger the PTSD. Not that it had been completely gone since I still wasn't sleeping much and taking two to three showers per day. I tried to hide the symptoms, but she would be the first to really see my broken self, not in its entirety yet more than I had ever allowed anyone to see.

Intimacy was certainly a challenge for me and consequently for us. We had (and still have) so much love and respect for each other that finding a compromise was easy. We are from a small town and it didn't take long for people to start talking about us. June 6, 1996, she left her husband of twenty-five years and moved in with me. Everything happened so fast I didn't have time to think about the whole situation which was probably a good thing. We went on weekend trips to get away from all the gossip. She was shunned by most of her friends except for a select few. I, on the other hand, didn't get that kind of treatment. I guess I come from a different generation and all my friends thought it was wonderful that I finally had met someone who made me happy.

I wish I could say we lived happily ever after, but that is never the case in real life. We would have many challenges and adventures along the way, and my PTSD took me to some pretty dark places within myself. I still struggled with those feelings of worthlessness, and shame, and for the longest time could not understand what she could possibly see in me. She once bought me a wall picture which still hangs in our home today, with this saying on it: "To the world you may be one person; but to one person you are the world", actually a quote by Dr. Seuss. Today I can say I get the meaning of those words and it certainly goes both ways. Without her I would not be the person I am today or most likely alive for that matter.

We purchased our first home in Bathurst in the fall of 1997 and this would be our home for a little more than eight years. I learned to landscape and in those years we built the most beautiful gardens. We spent all of our time outside and I guess playing in the dirt kept me grounded and functional. I would still get occasional flashbacks and these would mainly occur while standing at a store checkout. All of a sudden Denise would notice a strange look on my face and I'd say, "He's here. I can smell him", and sure enough I would look around and he would be at the next cash. Unfortunately, this would be something that I felt would never go away as long as I lived in the same city as my rapist.

I changed jobs during this time and took on a position with a bit more responsibility and challenge. Denise always backed me up on anything I ever wanted to do. She always believed that I was much smarter than I ever gave myself credit for, so now I was doing the work of a senior accountant. Accounting is something I seemed to know and I'm not sure why I do. I feel very gifted in this area and most of it is just logical to me. It's something that comes easy to me and I still enjoy working with numbers to this day.

I know this is kind of off topic, but there's something I need to bring up here. My monthly menstrual cycle had always been an issue for me. The severe cramping triggered the PTSD and every month the flashbacks would get worse. Again, taking extreme measures, I finally convinced my family doctor to refer me to a gynecologist as I wanted to get a hysterectomy and erase all possibility of constant monthly triggers. At that time none of my doctors were aware of the rape or any history of what my life had been like up to that point. I chose not to share that information with them. After several different attempts at trying to achieve my goal of surgery, the gynecologist finally agreed to a partial hysterectomy. I was now thirty-nine and had decided long ago I was never going to have children, so she scheduled the surgery which took place early September of 2004.

Recovery was a breeze and after a week I felt ready to go back to work. I had been out walking a bit and since I'd had laparoscopic surgery, there were no real scars to recover from or major stitches etc. On the seventh day after being released from the hospital, I told Denise while we were having supper that I didn't feel very well and assumed maybe I had overdone it a bit during the day. I decided to lay on the sofa for a bit and all I remember is that within about an hour she called an ambulance and I was rushed to the emergency. I was in excruciating pain. The gynecologist was called in and by this time I had developed a fever.

A general surgeon was also called in. I would find out later that he wasn't feeling very well that evening and wanted to wait until the next day before doing an explorative surgery to find out what was wrong with me. Luckily for me his instincts wouldn't allow him to walk away and go home that evening before doing a thorough check. I was brought into the operating room, put under general anesthesia while they opened up my abdomen. They discovered that I had been slowly dying from a massive infection. I was told that a mesh which was used to control the bleeding from the first surgery caused this infection due to a possible allergy to the material in it. Had he waited until the next day, they would not have been able to get to the infection on time. This time the recovery would be a bit more difficult. I'd had two surgeries within seven days. The antibiotics alone this time around were enough to make anyone sick.

My time in the hospital after the second surgery was horrible. I thought for sure I wasn't going to make it out of there. This time I had a large incision on my abdomen and the antibiotics smelled like cat pee. It would take almost a week before I could eat solid food. Denise came to see me every day and stayed with me for as long as I needed her there. She gave me the strength to fight and finally I was sent home where I recovered much faster.

Life eventually returned to normal, or as "normal" as my life had ever been. I had become convinced by this time that it was the price I had to pay for getting a surgery that I didn't medically need. After all I lied to get it, I had never told the Gynecologist about the rape or the PTSD. I understand today that I very much needed this surgery to survive emotionally, and yes, although it may seem extreme, I would do it all over again today if the same circumstances presented themselves. I also understand now that I needed to physically remove anything that would remind me of the rape hence the removal of most of my teeth, the breast reduction, and now the partial hysterectomy.

That would pretty much be it for me where surgeries were concerned. There really wasn't much left to take out of me besides my appendix.

CHAPTER 10
TASTE OF FREEDOM

The issues from this last surgery were a bit of a wakeup call for me. I was becoming disenchanted with my work and starting to think that maybe leaving the city might be a good option for me. It was getting really hard to go out and see him everywhere. I was reaching the point where I didn't really want to go out anymore and was starting to get somewhat depressed. Denise and I discussed possibly moving somewhere else, and in October 2005 we agreed to put our house on the market. Our house sold in February 2006 and we decided that Edmonton, Alberta would be our new destination. No specific reason why we chose it; we just picked a city where we knew I could easily get work. I was asked by my employer if I would delay the move and agree to work for them until the end of May. If I agreed they would pay all accommodations and living expenses due to having sold our house here and having no place to live in the interim.

We didn't really have anything waiting for us in Alberta, so Denise and I agreed to delay our leaving and moved into a hotel. We stayed for ten weeks and finally decided that April would be when we would move out west. All we were taking with us was about a dozen boxes which were to be shipped via Purolator and our clothes. Everything else we owned had been sold prior to us leaving our house. This was truly what one would call a fresh start. We shipped our car by train and booked our flights to Edmonton.

Finally our departure date arrived. I was excited and scared at the same time. This was my chance to start new. I remember being on the plane and big tears started streaming down my face. I wasn't sad; this was a moment I never thought I would see. I was now going to be free: never having to look over my shoulder, and never having to worry about him being in the same store at the same time as me. What a relief that was. For the first time in my life all my guards were down. Basically I was free to be anyone I wanted to be as no one knew us out there. It was truly a fresh start.

We had made enough money from the sale of our house to carry us for as long as needed. Denise's friend's daughter put us up for a week or two and showed us around the city. She helped us find a place to live, and we picked up our car and got established. We settled into a brand new apartment in the north end of the city. It had everything we needed within walking distance and we were a step away from the Light Rail Train which took us downtown. We got to shop for everything that we would need to start our new life there. Once we were able to pick up our car, we made our way around the city. For me, it was a magical and exciting time.

I met with a few temp agencies and within no time got a job with an accounting firm. I believe there is a reason for every person who comes into our lives and this man that I would be working for played an integral part in getting my own business off the ground. I will be forever grateful to him for his help. Every morning I hopped on the train and made my way downtown to one of those high rise buildings. Most of the staff was nice although there were a few who couldn't be bothered to even say hello, but I didn't care. It was so great to just feel good and finally be able to breathe.

Most of the downtown Edmonton is connected with inside tunnels and pathways, and at lunch time I used to just love going to one of the main points and sit there watching thousands of people rush by. I loved the fact that I didn't know any of them and better yet they didn't know me. What a sense of freedom. At the same time I should have felt lonely, but I didn't.

July 17, 2006, I took a full-time job as a controller with one of the firm's clients as I didn't want to work through a temp agency anymore. I worked full-time until October 20, 2006 for this company. I didn't find I was busy enough, so we agreed that I would continue to work for them on a contract basis. This allowed me to go back and work for the accounting firm on a contract basis as well. Between the two contracts I was able to make a good living and still have some flexibility with my time. I felt like I was finally in control of my life and was feeling a sense of accomplishment again. I was loving life again.

My mom and younger sister came to visit during that summer and we travelled to Jasper and visited the Edmonton Mall. It was nice of them to make the trip and I really enjoyed their visit. We rode the City Light Rail train and showed them around the city. It was a nice and relaxing time for me. It was pretty much a stress free life and I was enjoying every minute of it.

In October we flew back home for a week's visit since we missed our friends and family. We were able to spend time with everyone that was important to us. I really noticed how things had changed while we were away even if it was only six months. People's lives had moved forward just as ours had out west. You don't notice change when you are living in the middle of it, but when you're on the outside looking in you can see it.

On our return to Edmonton we landed in a blizzard. That was certainly a rare sight for us as we were not used to seeing snow in October and it took us a bit longer to get home. We arrived to a telephone message saying not to worry, but my dad was in the hospital as he had suffered a heart attack. I went to bed with a heavy heart that night and was only somewhat reassured after making a phone call to find out that he would recover. Although he was still in the Intensive Care Unit, I kept in touch by phone and my family kept me updated. I struggled with not being there, which again stirred up feelings that I wasn't a very good daughter. You know those nasty little voices that creep up on me every once in a while.

In the meantime, Denise had gotten a job at a grocery store and was meeting new people. Winters are long, cold, and dark in Edmonton, and if you're prone to depression it's not the best place to be. Denise had been taking medication for years for anxiety, but had never been properly treated. Over the winter she became more and more depressed and felt she was really missing her friends and life back home. I, on the other hand, loved Edmonton.

We flew to Kelowna, BC for Christmas hoping it would make it a bit more exciting for her and maybe help with her depression. We spent a few days there, but we eventually had to go back home to the cold and darkness of winter. Finally in March we decided that it would be better if we were to move back east. I knew she wasn't doing well and since I had not had any PTSD symptoms at all since we had left, I figured it would be okay for me to return as well. She mattered more to me than life itself so I had to make sure she was happy and would forgo my own happiness for hers.

Exactly a year to the day we had initially left the East Coast for Edmonton, we flew back home. We stayed with my parents until our furniture arrived. In the meantime, we found an apartment on a month to month lease as we knew we would be shopping for a house at some point in the near future.

House shopping kept us busy and I accepted a job with the company I had worked for prior to leaving. My first day of work was May 14, 2007, but it quickly became obvious to me that it was no longer what I wanted. Basically I had gotten used to the freedom of being my own boss and I didn't really care for the people I was working with at the company. I had grown accustomed to setting my own hours and was having a really hard time getting used to being around people who walked around hating everything about life and felt it necessary to complain all the time. Denise and I discussed it and she agreed that I would be miserable if I stayed there.

I suggested to my bosses that perhaps I could create an office in our home. That way I could work on my own and not have to deal with coworkers, but they didn't think they could work with that so I quit June 27, 2007 – the same day we signed all the legal papers to purchase our new house. Yes, we had found a house, and although it was a nice house, it would never become a home for me. And that wasn't due to the lack of trying on both our part. We immediately started working on the landscaping and redoing some of the interior, but doing those projects had lost its luster for me. I no longer enjoyed it as much and found it physically demanding as my body did not always cooperate since I never fully recovered from the back injury.

I had remained on contract as a part-time controller for one of the companies I'd worked for in Alberta. I was able to log in from home and monitor the books, and every three months I would travel to Edmonton for face to face meetings and ensure everything was going smoothly. I was still in touch with the people I had worked for our there and the accounting firm also agreed to hire me as a contract accountant. This meant I would be setup to work from home which allowed me to do a bit of marketing to see if I could get a few other clients. The money wasn't as consistent as a full-time job offered, but it was enough to keep us afloat. I was now effectively self-employed.

Financially this would be a source of stress for me for a long time. I wasn't sure I could make this work, but Denise had no doubt that we would be okay. I earned a bit less the first few years than I would have had I kept my full-time job yet we made it work. I spent many hours sending letters and emails advertising my services to prospective new clients. I've never been the kind of person to stay still and wait for something to fall in my lap. I believe hard work always pays off and that it did.

The contract with the accounting firm in Edmonton ended June 2008 when they merged with a major firm. Although not a surprise, it would still be a financial hit for me, but we would be okay. I still had the other controller contract and had managed to pick up a few smaller contracts along the way. Life kept moving forward.

CHAPTER 11
DARKNESS TO RENEWED HOPE

The stress of moving back to my hometown started to catch up with me. Slowly the nightmares and flashbacks returned. I would run into him on occasion and found that extremely difficult to deal with when it happened. I had hoped this was all behind me, but I was wrong. I found out later that PTSD can be somewhat dormant for long periods until it gets triggered by as little as just one memory, smell, or taste. I no longer had access to all those defense mechanisms I had put together to protect myself for years while living here. I had let most of them go when we moved to Edmonton and wasn't able to access them as easily as before. This wasn't necessarily a bad thing, but it would make life unbearable for me for a while.

Sleep became a luxury and I started losing weight. I also started losing my hair, lost all my eyebrows, and most of my eyelashes which are all signs of severe stress. Everything has since grown back with my eyebrows and eyelashes much lighter and they appear almost nonexistent. Yet I've learned to live with it and an eyebrow pencil can work wonders when needed. I started to notice that being in small spaces or in groups of people would cause me to panic and feel like I was suffocating. Heavy blankets on a bed or being in a dark bedroom also gave me that same feeling.

In October 2008 we decided to put the house on the market. I was offered a job in Amherst, NS with the option of living in Moncton. I truly wasn't doing very well being back in my hometown and knew I needed to move away. Denise wasn't aware of the extent of my stress and anxiety as I always tried to shelter her from it, but I was truly struggling. I figured as long as we stayed in New Brunswick she would be okay with the move. I was looking for a permanent job which would facilitate the move financially and give us time to get established somewhere else.

Somehow, even in my darkness moments, I knew I needed help, so I reached out to a local psychologist. We couldn't seem to agree on the type of treatment and parted ways after a few sessions. She didn't think she could offer much help. She expected me to just jump into the trauma starting at the second session without knowing anything about me, and I certainly didn't form that level of trust in that short of time with anyone. By this time I was truly overwhelmed with everything I was experiencing and becoming desperate. Suicide was once again an option considered on more than one occasion.

I spent a lot of time looking for contract work on the internet and came across a firm in Yellowknife that was hiring contract accountants for onsite work. We arranged for a telephone interview February 26, 2009 and I was hired. On March 4, I booked my flight to Yellowknife leaving April 11, 2009. This was a last desperate escape for me. I made sure all of my affairs were in order and that Denise would be taken care of. Yes, I was leaving knowing I was never coming back, at least not alive. I just couldn't handle everyday life anymore. At this point I figured that my life would always be shrouded in darkness. I had tried but just couldn't handle the flashbacks, nightmares, and anxiety anymore and to me I was out of options. Again I had failed.

I had lunches and coffee dates with as many people as I could over the next month. For me it was like I was saying goodbye. It was bittersweet, but there was an end in sight for me, and as odd as it sounds, believing that was comforting. The pain, hurt, fear, loneliness, isolation, self-hatred, blame, shame, and everything else I had accumulated over the years would finally be gone. I would be at peace.

I made it to Yellowknife. Things didn't get off to a very good start as the contact person that was to pick me up at the airport never showed up. After trying to get hold of her for over two hours, I finally got a taxi to take me to the nearest hotel. I was eventually able to reach her the next day. She picked me up and dropped me off at this dirty, substandard apartment. It was even smaller than what one would consider a bachelor suite to be with a mattress directly next to the refrigerator in the kitchen/living area. The bathroom had mildew at the bottom of the walls and it was like a sauna in there even if it was -40C outside. The heat was coming from the business below with no way of controlling it. This was to be home for the next twenty weeks. Maybe if I had been twenty-five or so I would have sucked it up and made the best of the situation, but at forty-four, I couldn't see myself living like that. Not sure why it mattered since I wasn't planning to stick around very long, but part of me seemed to not be quite ready to give up just yet.

I grabbed my stuff and moved into a hotel until myself and the company who'd hired me could agree on acceptable accommodations. Eventually it ended up costing me seven hundred dollars per month to stay and work there while they had initially said they would take care of these costs. It was the difference between the cost of the crappy apartment and the place I finally chose. I didn't really care as this was truly only temporary for me, but at the same time things were changing. I was in a strange place where once again no one knew me. I could breathe and was finally able to get some sleep.

It was nice to once again not have to look over my shoulder or worry about triggers. I showed up for work every day and worked as many hours as I could as it kept my mind busy. No matter where you are or who you are, people will always be put on your path for a reason, some nicer than others. As I mentioned before, there's something to be learned from everyone who comes into your path. Most of the people at work couldn't be bothered to give me the time of day except for one lady who was nice to me from day one. I think our offices were next to each other or maybe one office in between us. Either way it was easy to see what was going on in and around you.

The main partner of the firm wasn't a very nice guy. He was arrogant, insensitive, didn't have much of a personality, and was the type to pick on someone if he didn't like them. For some reason he was allowed to get away with this behaviour. We didn't really click and he stayed away from me, but I didn't care much for how he treated my co-worker who was now my friend. I happened to walk into her office one day and I could clearly see she was upset. We started to talk about life and she shared with me that she had a family member in rehab for drugs and alcohol, but the centre was kicking him out for breaking the rules and she didn't know what to do.

I shared with her the little bit that I knew about addiction along with my personal struggles with alcohol, and what generally happens to the families of addicts. That was the start to a very beautiful friendship. Actually, she would be one of those people that I consider my angels. Her friendship offered me a candle so that I could once again see the light at the end of the tunnel.

My world had gotten pretty dark and now I had another opportunity to keep fighting. I let her into my world a bit and she never judged or made me feel uncomfortable. She was seeing the real me which was not something I generally allowed. She didn't seem to think I was weird or odd, and if she did, she never showed it. I used to share jokes with her and one day someone posted one on Facebook that still makes us laugh today. It was something along these lines: "If life gives you lemons; you now have a choice. Make lemonade, or use them to squirt the juice into the eyes of people that piss you off." We were both thinking of the same person to use it on at the time.

When I left work that day, I stopped in at the grocery store and picked up a few lemons. The next morning I made sure to be there before her and placed one on her desk and one on mine. I think that bonded us for life. Yes, something as insignificant as a lemon can help cement a fabulous friendship. A few years later I received a package in the mail and it was a glass jar with plastic lemons in it. It still sits on my desk today. She would be the first person other than my psychologist who would get to read what I had written in prior years relating to the rape. That was a big deal for me as it meant that I would have to face this person the next day as I'd given her the pages of writing the night before. She never judged or gave me any reason to feel ashamed, but I still did. I would slowly overcome that the more time we spent chatting.

I talked to Denise everyday on the phone and low and behold, we got an offer on our house. That probably happened around my second week in Yellowknife. There was renewed hope for me. We talked about where we could live and settled on Moncton which was still in New Brunswick and within driving distance to everyone we wanted to stay close to. I was getting excited again, but scared at the same time. Would I be able to get back to a place that was bearable for me emotionally? I decided to try and contact the psychologist that had worked me when I was in my mid-twenties. I wasn't even sure if she still had a private practice so I called the number that I'd kept in my contacts list and left her a message. We played a bit of phone tag and I think we were finally able to connect by email. We agreed to meet May 29 when I would be back from up north. I think she knew I was on very shaky grounds and had readily agreed to see me.

By this time I had flown to a small hamlet in Nunavut to do some on site work there from May 3rd to the 18th. Everything seemed to be moving really fast which is not a bad thing for someone like me, since the less time I have on my hands to sit and analyze things, the better I do. The closing on our house was May 28th. I was scheduled to arrive back home on May 24th. I had managed to get movers lined up, a hotel booked for when we got to Moncton, and in the meantime Denise found us an apartment. What a small world we live in. I'm thousands of miles from my hometown and the first person I meet is from the same hometown as me, plus her husband was from Fredericton, NB, a nearby city. Even though we didn't know each other it was still somewhat of a comfort just knowing they were from my part of the country.

My last official work day for that firm was May 21st. I could tell from my last meeting with the boss that I would more than likely have problems getting paid what I was owed, and I was right. The fact that it would take a year to collect my last paycheque shows the type of people I was dealing with while working for that firm. It would take me filing a lawsuit in small claims court to finally collect the seven thousand dollars they owed me. However, it also proves that I will do everything I possibly can before giving up on something. I knew I had done good work for them and had fulfilled my contract. I wasn't about to kiss that amount of money goodbye without a fight.

I ended up leaving Yellowknife a few days earlier than previously planned, so I stayed a few nights in Edmonton with an old friend before catching my final flight home. It gave me a chance to gather my thoughts a bit before heading back. I knew I needed to make sure I had a good support system around me as I didn't trust myself. I knew that suicide isn't always a planned thing, and that if it got dark enough in my head it would only take a split second for me to do something I couldn't come back from and that scared me.

We finally settled in Moncton and I kept seeing the psychologist every few weeks for about a year. That's how long it took for me to feel safe within myself again. The period leading to us moving to Moncton had left me pretty beaten up emotionally.

Work was finally picking up and I was getting a few more contracts which kept my mind busy. I've always used work as an escape and generally love getting lost in it. The next little while would be up and down for me as I slowly crept out of that dark hole I had been in. I realized once again that there was hope after all. I was still having major issues with anxiety and these would last up to three weeks without reprieve, generally leaving me gasping for air most of the time. Sometimes just being me was exhausting.

CHAPTER 12
FOUNDATION TO HEALING

My psychologist suggested we make an appointment to see someone who would more than likely be able to help me breathe better. I was willing to try almost anything at this point, so she made an appointment for mid-August 2009 with a respiratory therapist. I don't remember much of the session except that I could, for the first time in a long time, catch my breath. She showed me a few techniques to help relax the muscles in my throat that had grown so tense over the years which helped me breathe better. I also left there a bit more relaxed.

I was to see her again the following week and would continue to work with her regularly. She became a trusted friend who has been there to help me through the rough times and enjoy the good times. We remain good friends today. We would eventually have the opportunity to travel together to various places across Canada and the US.

My friend, the respiratory therapist, met up with me in Edmonton February 2010 while I was on one of my regular trips, and we flew out to Yellowknife. It had been nine months since I had left there and was really looking forward to seeing my friend. She was now pregnant with her first child and was radiant. We had a wonderful visit and it was good for me to see how far I had come since the last time I was there. I was somewhat sad to leave simply because it was a positive experience for me to return there. I would over the next several years have the opportunity to return which I will tell you about in a latter chapter.

The next few months were relatively quiet and in early June I was off to Edmonton again for work. My friend, the respiratory therapist, would fly up once again to meet me there and from there we went to Whitehorse, Yukon, and Southern Alaska. The north is by far my favorite place in the world; a place I would revisit on more than one occasion throughout the years. It's a place where I seem to be able to allow myself to feel everything around me. I was able to be in the moment, something that had eluded me all of my life. The Rocky Mountains are breathtaking. This is a place where I can feel grounded: the water, eagles, grizzly bears, mountains, and the fresh air. I felt totally at peace there and often wished I could have bottled that feeling.

People have often asked why we just didn't move there. I don't think that would be a wise thing for me to do. I'm naturally prone to isolating myself when things start to unravel a bit and that could be dangerous for me. I've worked really hard at not living in my own little world, but I don't think it would take very much for me to go there again. Denise would not be one to live in a place so isolated either. I've learned to create that world around me, a haven I call home where I can find that feeling and be in the moment. It takes some work and a lot of practice, at times more so than others, but it has become a part of my daily routine.

Life went back to a relatively normal state. Some of my contracts required a little more travel than others. My part-time controller contract came to an end in March 2011 when the company became a Crown Corporation. It was hard to say goodbye to some of my co-workers as I had worked alongside them for five years now and I had grown to like some of them very much. I knew that this would mean we would part ways and more than likely never see each other again. I often think of them and did share part of my story with two of them a few years later.

I had the opportunity from April to early June 2011 to work in Summerside, PEI. If you recall I had briefly lived there at the height of my alcoholism and now it was a chance to revisit. I remembered very little from that time and not much looked familiar to me. I was also able to get in touch with the person who had taken the time to try and help me some twenty-eight years prior. I was now twenty-seven years sober and was heartbroken to find out she had not been able to maintain any amount of sobriety and was still struggling with alcohol. I will be forever grateful to have had her in my life at that time as she had played a big part in changing the path my life was on. We have stayed in touch through Facebook and I think of her often.

I was twelve years sober the last time I attended an Alcoholics Anonymous meeting and don't feel that I would be able to help someone get sober today. It's just not where I am anymore and I have moved on. Some would say I've forgotten where I came from, but obviously from this book, that is not the case. I simply chose to move on and live the principles I've learned during my time there. Alcohol for me had always been a symptom or a way to mask deeper issues. I don't believe I was born an alcoholic; I became one due to events and circumstances in my life. I've been working on these issues for years now and no longer think or need alcohol when life becomes problematic.

I also had the opportunity to make a trip back to the Yukon and Alaska in mid-June of 2011. This time I would be able to share this beautiful journey with my parents. My dad had always wanted to see the Yukon, Dawson City in particular, so my friend and I made sure this would be part of our trip. We spent eight days together and it was very nice to be able to spend that time with them. I can't say that we've ever been close as secrets have a tendency to create distances between people. It was just nice to be with them and to have a chance to get to know them. At this point I was also learning to let my guard down a bit. The feelings I had the first time I visited this place were so vivid in my memory and it was wonderful to once again be able to just be. The midnight sun, fresh air, mountains, wildlife, and the water still bring a sense of well-being to my soul, even to this day.

Though everything seemed to be falling into place in my life, I was always left with this hole that could never be filled. I often wondered if I would ever feel whole again. I would every once in a while step into the world of emotions, but generally I just avoided feeling too much of anything. Emotions were always very overwhelming for me and I can understand why today. For the better part of my life I lived in what I refer to as my logical side of the brain where emotions rarely come into play and everything is always on an even keel: no major ups or downs, but no joy or sadness either, leaving only emptiness. It's something that I still feel on occasion and may never quite get rid of.

January 2012 would take me once again to Yellowknife for work. I had secured a contract with a local firm there. From there I would be flown into the small community of Trout Lake, population 119. On all of my trips I would meet amazing people who would change my life in some way. Here I met a young woman who like me had battled with alcoholism and she too, had been sexually abused. She shared with me how her community stood behind her when she chose to make the perpetrator accountable. She testified and he was found guilty. All I could think about while listening to her was how strong and courageous she was to take that step. I would surely never be able to do that. I was there for about two weeks and learned a lot about their culture as she was an indigenous person. I've always admired the spirituality of Native and Inuit people.

At the end of my two weeks I made my way back to Fort Simpson. I was flying back from Trout Lake that morning and had a few hours to spare so I decided to have breakfast a local hotel. What I hadn't realized was that I was at least a twenty minute drive from the airport and the town only had one taxi. The hotel had called him earlier but weren't able to reach him. I guess it must have started to show on my face that I was starting to panic a bit and it was becoming obvious I would not make it to the airport on time for my flight which meant I would also miss my connecting flight back home leaving Yellowknife the next morning.

There were quite a few people in the restaurant and one of them got up and offered to take me to the airport. He even called the airport to tell them we were on our way and to please hold the flight. I was really grateful and surprised that a complete stranger would do that for me. We talked about the Northern Lights and when the best time of year was to see them. We chatted like we knew each other and suddenly we had arrived at the airport. I tried to pay him for going out of his way, but he wouldn't take it. He wished me well and off I went. I never did get his name, but I will never forget him or my travels to the Grand North. Helping each other is a way of life and survival there and I truly felt comfortable in that environment.

If there's one thing I've learned through my travels in this life, it's that nothing is ever a coincidence. People come in and out of our lives to teach us something while some will leave a scar. On this day I learned that I was able to trust this person, yes, a man, and I wasn't afraid. That was a very powerful lesson for me. I had allowed myself to trust a total stranger.

One dream that I've yet to fulfill is seeing the Northern Lights. Of course, as soon as I say this, people send me emails with pictures or post them on Facebook, but it's not the same. I want to be able to feel the energy in the air while they dance in the sky, because to me it represents something very spiritual. I remember some of the children in Trout Lake were on the lookout for them and were told if they saw any to come and get me. They came to see me one evening, but the skies would never be clear enough to be able to see them. The children shared with me their belief that you can make the lights dance. It was magical to watch the children and be in the moment, something I could see but never able to hang onto for very long.

It's been an ongoing joke with my friends in the North. As soon as I would leave there I would receive emails saying that had I stayed just one more day I would have seen them. I've gone to what some would say are extreme measures to view these elusive Lights, planning trips just to see them. I have come to realize that someday, when I least expect it, I will see them.

I seemed once again to be searching for something or quite possibly trying to run away from myself. Either way, my travelling was increasing and I would be away quite a bit between January and June 2012. Some of the travelling was for work as I had not yet been able to find enough contracts to be able to work from home or locally. Early March brought a trip to Arizona and the Grand Canyon. I found myself getting a bit stressed and tired of the travelling but ignored those feelings. Once again I wouldn't listen to what my body and spirit was telling me.

April and May would be another opportunity for a three week work contract in Yellowknife where I would once again fly into Fort Simpson. The people I get to meet amaze me as they always share with me parts of their personal lives that show me how resilient and strong people can be. I always leave with significantly more self-knowledge than when I arrived. They treat you like royalty and invite you into their homes like you had known each other for years. I was given the grand tour and happened to be there just as the Mackenzie River ice decided to break open. I was only a few hundred feet from the river and could hear it crack and break open in the night.

Nature seems to always be part of my travels whether it be the Northern Lights, rivers, wildlife, or snow storms. It's all such a gift and uncontrollable at the same time. You really see how small you are in this vast universe. There was a high risk of flooding in Fort Simpson if the ice jammed further down the river so I left a few days earlier than expected. The Mackenzie River is the largest and longest river system in Canada and the force of the moving ice and water was amazing. I still have the videos that I took of the ice moving out. Was it a coincidence that I was there at that very moment? I don't think so. To be able to see all the amazing changes that occurs in nature and all its beauty is truly a gift.

My business was finally taking off and I was getting busier, which is what I wanted. I had one more trip booked for early June 2012. It would be the last trip my friend and I would make together. I think we were both a bit stressed with where we were in our lives, and unlike the other trips we had taken together, this one pushed my stress level above and beyond what I was able to handle. We spent many hours driving which I'm not a fan of at the best of times. Actually, I get very nervous in a car which is probably related to the three car accidents that I've had. We both got a bit frustrated and decided shortly after this trip that we wouldn't be travelling together anymore. Maybe it was an indication for me to move into another direction.

It wasn't necessarily a bad thing as it gave me a chance to get grounded a bit and see what it was I needed to do for me. It was time for Denise and me to travel together for a bit, so off we went to Vegas in September 2012. Obviously, I was doing much better financially which made it easy for us to travel. You can easily get lost in all the hustle and bustle of Vegas as it's like being in another world with the lights, shows, casinos, and the people in the "city that never sleeps." We had a room facing the Bellagio Fountains which lit up at night. I was actually very comfortable and happy there. In fact, we would travel to Vegas again the following April in 2013.

I now had a home office where I worked daily. I prefer to work alone. I found that office politics and the different dramas and personalities were overwhelming to me and at times frustrating. I'm not sure I'm meant to be around people that much. I can handle being in crowds but only in smaller doses. Being at home creates a feeling of security for me. I seem to get less triggers and it keeps the PTSD under control. My sleep can still be erratic and having a home office allows me the flexibility of working while most people sleep. I find it very productive and generally do my best work from 4:30 am until about 2:00 pm. In fact, working from home allowed me to tailor my work to fit all my quirks and what some would call disabilities.

In September 2013, Denise and I decided that maybe it was time for us to buy a house and make Moncton our permanent home. We had been there since 2009 and were doing quite well. It was a comfortable place for both of us. Although I had said many times I wasn't interested in owning another house, it became apparent to me that now at sixty-five it was important for Denise to feel settled and be able to get back into gardening. We moved into our new home October 11th, 2013. I now had an amazing office space and the house was perfect for us. We set it up to our liking and settled right in. It was a decision I have never regretted.

It turned out that 2014 would be a very busy year for me. I finally broke the hundred thousand dollar earnings target I'd set for myself. I thought if I was ever able to reach that goal, it would make me a successful person. You see, I still battled with low self-esteem and I thought of myself as basically uneducated. All I had was a High School diploma and when I looked at the people around me, I felt I didn't fit. I wasn't as "good" or as "smart" as they were, yet many of them weren't making a six figure salary. That fact didn't seem to matter as the bottom line was no matter what I accomplished, I was still left feeling that I was simply damaged goods and nothing would ever change that.

Yet, I was by all of today's standards, a successful business woman. I had a beautiful home, a new car, and an amazing partner who believed in me more than I ever could. I was able to travel and privileged to be able to do just about anything we wanted. By all accounts I had the perfect life. I had it made, yet I had this hole that I just couldn't seem to fill. That damn hole kept rearing its ugly head. That emptiness left by the feeling that nothing is ever going to be good enough to erase that my feelings of brokenness. I was tired of forever feeling broken.

CHAPTER 13
AN AMAZING TEAM

October 2014 would be the beginning of a life changing few years which brought me to now as I write this book. One day while visiting my parents, I came to realize during a general conversation with them that for years I had thought the first person I saw the morning after the rape was a nanny. I had never been able to put a face on the person that came to get me that morning; the only thing I knew was that it had been a woman. During our talk, I found out that we no longer had a nanny by the time I started school, so that left only one possibility as to the identity of that person: it had to be my mother.

I became really angry at that thought and then sad. Actually I was caught up in a mixture of all kinds of emotions, some I'm not sure I'd ever felt before. How could it be my mother? Should she not have said nor done something? Was I that horrible of a child that I didn't deserve to be defended and protected? At the same time part of my logical brain understood why she was unable to give me what I needed at the time. We were in a generation where these things were never talked about and generally swept under the rug. People didn't know what do to or how to handle the subject of rape or molestation. It is not my place to discuss what I may or may not think what my mother's issues were, but she also came with her own baggage of unresolved issues from her childhood trying to manage three small children, a job, a home and a husband let alone her own history.

This was a big trigger for me and the flashbacks and nightmares came back with a vengeance. I knew it was time for me to do whatever it took to finally deal with this and hopefully heal. I reached out to a friend that I had met in the late eighties who as a therapist. We had stayed in touch on and off throughout the years and I thought that since she knew bits and pieces of my story it would be easier working with her than starting over with a complete stranger.

We agreed to meet in early November. Our sessions would be via Skype since we didn't live in the same city let alone the same province. You have to like technology. It certainly facilitates life in a lot of areas. Emotions became very intense and often we would have sessions twice a week to try and get my anxiety under control. Everything seemed very raw and there weren't any buffers to tamper down the pain. I jumped in with both feet and when panic set in I'd jump back out to the sidelines by shutting down again.

It was important to surround myself with people that I knew could help me and be somewhat part of a team of professionals I could have access to in order to get better. My team included only women. That was a personal choice made by me. I knew that the issues I needed to deal with would be very painful and uncomfortable, and it was important for me to feel like I was in control of this part of my healing.

This team included my family doctor who is absolutely amazing. She is very compassionate and was the first doctor I ever told my story to. I was now almost fifty and none of the physicians who had ever treated me knew of the sexual assaults or what my life had been like in the past. She has been a great supporter through this entire process and actually had her receptionist call me to setup an appointment just to see how I was doing. I am so fortunate to have people like her as part of my team. During my last visit to see her she just sat there and we talked for over an hour. I've never had a family physician that would even bother to do that. I can tell she genuinely cares.

I also have a massage therapist, my friend who is my psychotherapist, and a respiratory therapist who has studied in all kinds of healing therapies as part of my team. This group of amazing women have allowed me to be who I needed to be and respected my journey as well as challenged me when I needed it. I've been able to build trust with people on a level that was never attainable for me until now. This group grew and some of the team members changed over the course of the next few years as I made my way through my healing journey. But all of these wonderful people remained very much a part of my healing process.

I allowed myself to share with them what it had been like for me and my battle with anxiety, depression, addiction, and PTSD. Sometimes the only way I was able to do that was in writing. It seems easier for me to write it down than to talk about it face to face, although I am getting better at talking. Some of the events in my life I can still only share in writing. I'm not really sure why saying the words feel so overwhelming for me that my brain just shuts down, but I accept my limitations for now and try to challenge them from time to time.

Sometime in early February or March 2015, I started thinking about possibly filing a lawsuit against the guy that raped me when I was seven. I didn't know if it was even possible at this stage, but I wanted to pursue it further. By this time, my younger sister and I had talked a bit and I knew he had also done something to her. I had suspected that for about twenty years, but we never discussed it or at least not that I remember. I turned fifty in April and I thought it was time for me to finally take this step. It was my birthday gift to myself. My sister and I decided that we would go into this together. I put a brief email complete with all the pertinent information and sent it off to several lawyers who dealt in civil law.

We finally chose a lawyer in Moncton who is very knowledgeable in sexual abuse cases. I was surprised and impressed at the fact that he was very gentle and compassionate during all of our meetings. It's not something I was expecting, especially from a man. Please don't think that I'm "male bashing" here as I'm not. Keep in mind that almost all my experiences to date with men had not been very good to say the least. I sent him all the information I had in writing and things progressed very quickly from our initial meeting. I had met with him June 23, 2015, and he spoke to my sister two days later. By the end of June both of our claims had been filed with the Court and the defendant was served July 6, 2015.

For me, this was a major step forward. I knew that even if nothing came of the suit it would at least force me to confront the issue head on. It came as a relief to my family as well. Unbeknownst to me they had known of the rape for many years now, but no one knew how to approach the subject. As for me, at least now the secret was out. I wouldn't have to walk on egg shells and watch everything I said or did anymore when around them for fear of saying something that would give away my secret. I wouldn't have to look over my shoulder anymore either for fear of running into him.

I had also reached the point that I needed to do this for me. My intention has never been, nor will it ever be, to deliberately hurt my family or others around me. This is simply how I lived and perceived the events around me and my perceptions may not necessarily agree with those of others. My family and I speak in very general terms relating to the lawsuit and some of the events, but I can't see that I will ever be comfortable discussing more of it with my family. I've always had support systems around me that excluded them and I prefer to keep it that way.

Even if it was finally time for all of this to be out in the open, I still felt a tremendous amount of stress, shame and anxiety with the process. My focus now was to get ready for the discovery hearing. This meant that I had to be able to tell three other people plus a court reporter what he had done to me. That thought alone was enough to cause an anxiety attack. It would certainly push me beyond any level of comfortability I had ever imagined.

I made sure I stayed busy with work because it occupies my mind and keeps me grounded. I still received psychotherapy on a weekly basis along with massages when needed to relax my muscles. My sleep was a bit more erratic than usual, but I managed and I would often have a nap in the afternoon to make sure I stayed functional.

I kept myself surrounded by people who knew what was happening and who were supportive of this process. At this point I had shared this step of my journey with probably thirty or more people. It was important for me to include as many people as I was comfortable with telling about what was had happened to me and what was going to happen in the near future. It was a way for me to remain accountable and see this through till the end.

When I told my friend in Yellowknife what I had decided to do, I received a pair of handmade moccasin slippers in the mail with a beautiful card of encouragement. This gesture of kindness carried me through the next phase of my journey. I also took it as symbol that she would be walking with me the whole way. It was by far the most precious thing anyone had ever done for me. I wore them out and when I could no longer wear them I put them in a shadow box and hung them on my wall as a reminder of the support around me.

In early July I came across a pamphlet advertising a trip to Iceland to see the Northern Lights. As you all know it's always been a dream of mine to see them and even after several trips to Northern Canada I had yet to see them. So after some discussion with Denise, I decided to go. It would be good for me to get away as it had been a pretty stressful year. There was a group of people going on this trip. No one that I knew, but I decided to go just the same. I figured I would surely fit in somewhere and if I didn't feel like socialising I wouldn't have to. We left October 1st and returned the 8th.

It was a nice trip but unfortunately, it rained the entire time we were there so that meant no Northern Lights. I met some really nice people and managed to fit in relatively well. I did some sightseeing around the city of Reykjavik and went on a few organized tours. The break was nice and allowed me to step away from the level of intensity my day to day life had become.

Gambling at times became an issue and a way of coping that I used frequently. I found that the noise and the lights were a way to shift my focus away from the issues at hand. Gambling certainly engaged the senses and helped calm some of the flashbacks. Of course, the good feeling was short lived when I would actually look at how much money I'd lost, and again I would beat myself up for being weak and stupid. Money didn't seem to have any value to me. After doing a quick calculation, I easily lost twenty-five thousand dollars in twelve months. I'm certainly not happy with that, but I understand the reasons for doing it and was fortunate to be financially secure enough for it not to seriously impact us. It's certainly not a behavior I could afford to maintain and decreased the number of visits to the casino once I realized what I was doing.

I should also add that I'm very much an emotional eater and have easily gained twenty-five to thirty pounds since starting this process. I try not to beat myself up too much over this as I also realize it's very much a coping mechanism for me. I've always been overweight, but this is my heaviest. It's not a comfortable weight for me and it's causing some physical problems. My blood pressure has been a bit hard to control and my back is struggling to handle the excess weight which creates other problems. I'm not very disciplined when it comes to exercise and have used that as an excuse. I know I have the strength to get this under control but it would have to wait until the trial is over.

As per my agenda book, it looks like we increased the therapy sessions to twice a week until the end of April. I was growing more and more aggravated and agitated at my inability to talk and everything seemed to be triggering me. We finally had received tentative dates for the Discovery Hearing to be held the week of October 24, 2016. I think trying to force things to happen and relive it all the time created an extreme amount of stress until I finally shut down. I just didn't want to do it anymore. We had done a tremendous amount of work, but I needed to take a step back. I walked away from therapy for the time being.

I was overwhelmed by the flood of emotions and actively engaged in coping mechanisms that were not the best for me. Yes, I'm talking about gambling and eating. I realize today that it allowed me to get through to the next chapter. I also understand more and more that how you get to the point of resolution is not as important as actually getting there. This might come across as an excuse to some, but at the same time I managed to get where I needed to be.

In May 2016 as I was updating my profile on LinkedIn, an online resource site for professionals, I came across the name of a social worker in the city I live in who worked specifically with PTSD and trauma victims and it sparked my curiosity. So I sent her an email and we agreed to meet May 24, 2016, after Denise and I returned from Vegas where we celebrated our twentieth anniversary. Yes, imagine that. I had been in a relationship for twenty years. Me, the broken one no one could possibly love, the one that would be alone forever. I called this a miracle and truly feel what it's like to be loved when I allow myself to be in the moment. Not something I've been able to master yet and make it part of my everyday living, but it's something I strive to be able to accomplish.

I sent the social worker some of my writings before meeting with her since it's a bit hard to try and explain all the dynamics in play from day one, especially starting from scratch with someone you have never met before. We met weekly up to October 20th. The following Monday was to be the start of the discovery hearing, but I received an email from my lawyer on the fourteenth that the hearing would be cancelled and pushed to the spring of 2017. The reason for the postponement is not important and there would be several postponements, none of which were requested by us. I realize now that these all worked out in my favor and afforded me more time to get ready.

To say I was upset about the hearing being postponed would be an understatement. I was so angry. For months I had been working to prepare myself for it and then poof! – it was cancelled. I do have to admit now that he did me a favor as I'm not sure I was quite ready for it. I've come to the conclusion that I will probably only ever discuss what he did to me once when I was seven and that will be at the hearing. I no longer feel that discussing it is a requirement to my healing as I've been able to tell people about it via my writing.

Working towards the hearing date left me feeling very anxious. During the therapy sessions with the social worker I learned what happens to the brain after a trauma and was also given a few tools and exercises to help keep me grounded when my anxiety level would get out of control,. I learned about retraining the brain on how it reacts to the trauma when specific things are brought up as well. I would also have to agree that I'm in a "fight or flight" mode pretty much one hundred percent of the time which is why my sleep patterns are so erratic.

I also consulted with my family doctor during this period when the anxiety became a bit too intense. She, along with my therapist, strongly suggested I take something to help control the anxiety which would also help me to sleep and function better. I agreed to a very small dosage of anti-depressants which I took maybe a dozen times at the most. For reasons that are obvious, I need to be in full control of my mind and body all the time so taking anti-anxiety medications or sleeping pills is very difficult for me. I need to know that I can wake up in the middle of the night if need be. The medication was an option but not one that I relied upon.

In late September I decided to try acupuncture to see if it would help with the anxiety. I figured I'd also let her in on what was going on so she knew what she was dealing with when trying to treat me. It's helped a great deal with the anxiety, but trying to get the rest of my body to relax is a whole other story. It seems like that might take a lifetime as my body doesn't seem to be getting the message that it's safe now to let go of this fight or flight mode. My muscles get very tense from being in this state, sometimes to the point where I can barely lift up my arms or bend down to put on my socks. We continue to work on that and I do see some improvements, even if it's only for a few days at a time.

I had the opportunity to attend a workshop by Dr. Gabor Mate, a renowned speaker on topics such as addiction, stress and childhood development, on November 1 and 2, 2016 on trauma and addiction. His talk certainly explained the origin of all the coping mechanisms I'd developed over the years and how they had kept me alive. He explained trauma and addiction in a very logical way which made it easier for me to understand what I needed to take with me from that workshop. I was hoping he would also be able to tell me what the best treatment is for people like me, but he didn't. He spoke of several different treatments and therapies, where I learned basically one size doesn't fit all. So you keep trying until you find one that fits your particular situation. I felt I was in pretty good hands while I was there. I had my respiratory therapist friend sitting on one side of me, the social worker who is helping me with the PTSD on the other, and the psychologist that worked with me in my mid-twenties and again when we first moved to Moncton, a few tables behind me. It was like being wrapped in a security blanket.

Mid November I received a call from my doctor's office. The receptionist said the doctor would like to see me. I figured she wanted to see how I was doing. She would not have known that the hearing was cancelled. I went in to see her on November 28 and we chatted for about an hour. It was really nice to feel like she genuinely cared and was invested in making sure I was doing well. She was very excited to hear I was now writing a book. She had mentioned in previous visits that I really should think about doing that.

The anxiety decreased significantly in subsequent months and things quieted down. My sleep was still somewhat erratic at times and the anxiety did flare up, but it didn't last or upset me as much anymore. I continued working on myself with the help and support of the people around me. The flashbacks were rare at this point as I'd learned to deal with them better. I felt a bit more alive as I'd learned to allow my emotions to take their proper place in my life.

Writing this book has been a big part of my healing. While doing this, I felt like I was on the outside looking in at the situation, and so many pieces of the puzzle fell into place. It has made me a much stronger person. I've realized that the light is no longer flickering at the end of the tunnel, and maybe someday I'll be able to pass on a candle to someone else who is struggling with PTSD, addictions, and childhood sexual abuse. It is a lifelong battle, but I can say now it gets easier with every step.

I'm not sure what I'm expecting from the Discovery Hearing as it's never been about money for me. It was the only legal option available to me. Do I need to finally confront him after all these years and say I'm not afraid of him anymore? Will that bring me some sort of peace? Only time will tell. Will I ever forgive him? Not in this lifetime.

I'm looking forward to seeing what the next chapter will hold for me. I have renewed hope that I will be able to move on and built a meaningful life as I continue on my journey.

CHAPTER 14
THE NEXT CHAPTER

It is now one year later and the Discovery Hearing has been once again postponed until September 2018. I was told that this is it, the last postponement, and if they are unable to make it to the hearing, it will strike his defence and the case will go directly to the judge.

It has been a year of growth, pain, discovery, and new adventures. I continued to work with the Social Worker in preparation for the discovery hearing. I still found myself overwhelmed with the thought of having to share the details of the rape with those three men and a court stenographer.

I spent many hours in therapy and still, as I am writing, have not been able to openly discuss the trauma I experienced as a child. My brain seems to think that as long as I don't verbalize it, it can remain a story, and for me emotions are not attached to stories.

I've had the opportunity to be part of what some would call a healing ritual (one of many) as part of my therapy which would be the beginning of another amazing journey for me. It might sound childish and may even be stupid to some, but I will try to put it into words.

While in a therapy session, the point of the exercise was to transfer negative emotions that would rise during the session into a pebble or small stone that I would hold in my hand. I know the concept alone seems a bit out there, but I was asked to just try and trust the process. I would then drop this stone into a small pot containing Epsom salts and alcohol and prior to the end of the session my therapist would light the container which held the stones on fire and allow it to burn for a few minutes. This exercise was to symbolize the release of these emotions. Once the stones were cooled they were collected and put into a small sachet.

My therapist and I did this over a few sessions and during this time I received a request from a friend asking if I would be available for a short work contract requiring me to travel to Yellowknife. Would I call this a coincidence? Again I think not. It's like my journey was coming full circle. The very first time I was in Yellowknife was to die and now I had the opportunity to return while at a very different place in my life. My therapist thought this would be the perfect place to throw away all of my gathered stones as a symbolic sign of leaving those emotions behind.

Off I went on the trip with my little bag of stones, a bit apprehensive but excited at the same time. I was unsure how and where I would get rid of them, and at the same time I was feeling a bit stupid for believing that throwing these little stones away would change anything. I was greeted at the airport by my friend and one of her daughters. It felt good to be back and to see my friend who had such an impact on my life when we first met several years before. I was very much in a different place this time.

I settled in nicely and was looking forward to getting my work started. Over the next few days I met a beautiful little girl who was just a few months shy of seven, my friend's oldest daughter. Had you asked me what a seven-year-old looked like prior to this I would not have been able to answer. She would become my teacher this week and through her eyes I was able to see what a seven-year-old sees and how naive, trusting and carefree they truly are. I had never allowed myself to be that present before.

During this week I took a chance and shared the meaning of my little bag of stones with my friend. It's very new for me to allow myself to be vulnerable yet being far from home and with someone that I felt had never judged me made it easier. As stupid as I thought it would sound, I shared the task I was asked to complete with her. I found myself asking if she thought her daughter could share this task with me as well. Without any real planning, it all came together. The day prior to my leaving we made our way to the Pilot's Monument.

This monument is a lookout point overseeing large sections of the city of Yellowknife. The little girl was full of life as we made our way up the never ending stairs to the top. She was having fun. We stood at the top and I asked her if she could help me throw these little stones away that I was carrying in my little pouch. I stood next to her and watched as she threw most the stones as far as she could. I couldn't help but feel her energy. This was very overwhelming to me. I stayed a bit behind as they made their way back down the stairs and took my time coming back down for fear I would break down and cry. I'm not sure I could describe what I felt at that very moment only that it was very strong and, of course, uncomfortable for me.

Upon my return, I found myself questioning a lot of things. It didn't make sense to me that what I remembered could have happened to someone so small and innocent. I struggled with this thought for many months. I started to question my memories and once again struggled with anxiety. I became very angry and frustrated with myself and even questioned whether I should continue with the trauma work. I started to shut down again and coasted for a bit.

I'm inquisitive and curious by nature which allows me to be open to different things. Shortly before going to Yellowknife I met with a Shaman, (yes, I do believe some people have abilities and are what I would consider healers.) I have met many throughout the years that are mediums, psychics, and healers. They always provided me some comfort in knowing everything would be alright as long as I just kept doing what I was doing. Maybe it is all wishful thinking, but it works for me.

I believe we are surrounded by angels – some in human form and some in spirit form, from which we gain strength to continue on our journey. This past year I discovered that I was what is known as an empath. "Being an empath is when you are affected by other people's energies, and have an innate ability to intuitively feel and perceive others. You are always open, so to speak, to process other people's feelings and energy, which means that you really feel, and in many cases take on the emotions of others."

I found the possibility of being an empath really interesting and spent a bit of time exploring this on the internet as well as discussing it openly with a few people surrounding me who I've come to understand are also empaths. I also realized that I always seek out people who have these abilities. I know they understand without requiring an explanation. I'm one of those people that seem to know things but can't explain why I know, I just do. It also explains why I have never paid much attention to someone's outer appearance and always had the ability to sense what is going on behind the scenes. I thought I had become really good at reading people over the years. It's always been a part of me and I realize this trait more and more as I allow myself to be open to it. I've also used this to deflect attention from myself when interacting with people by simply asking them a few questions based on the energy I get from them. It's been a very beneficial tool for me. Even with all this knowledge about myself, I still find it difficult at times to understand the world around me.

I can easily get sidetracked and lost in my thoughts as I'm very much a person who lives in my head. I need things to make sense, otherwise I struggle with them. Understanding why something happens or what makes people do what they do is a really difficult task for me and often questions I have are left unanswered.

Whenever I feel like I'm in my head too much I try to keep myself somewhat grounded in the here and now by doing small things I remembered hearing while in therapy. Things such as spending time watching the birds gather in the backyard or going for a walk, I was told I lighten up when I speak about birdwatching so it's obviously something that offers me comfort. I do put out several feeders to ensure they continue to visit, and have a bird bath and fountain which attracts them as well. I spend many hours over the summer months observing them.

In this past year I've been able to share my writings with friends and family and I've been somewhat taken aback by their response. Strong, courageous, resilient, and successful were words commonly used by them after reading my story. I was truly surprised as these would not be words I would have ever used to describe myself. I am slowly starting to see what they see and continue to seek a better understanding of who I am.

We often hear that in adversity we find strength. What most people would consider disabling or roadblocks for me is simply finding a new way of adapting my life around it. Things such as becoming unable to function in a standard office environment or in a typical nine to five job have given me a wonderful gift. It has allowed me to build a successful business out of my home that meets all of my needs and in which I can flourish. I now live a very quiet but self-sustainable life.

Some would say I have a sleeping disorder and it would be difficult for me to argue the point since I rarely ever sleep more than an hour at a time. However, I chose to adapt to it rather than trying to treat it with medication. Being self-employed has been a blessing, allowing me to work as little or as many hours as I want when most people are fast asleep. And if I need a nap in the afternoon, I can do that since I work from home.

Visiting family and friends for an overnight stay used to be stressful and awkward due to my sometimes disruptive sleeping habits. I tend to putter around the house at night getting water, watching TV, and playing on my computer. Using hotels when visiting with family or friends has offered a simple fix as well as giving me the privilege of meeting people I would otherwise never get to know. The front desk employees are generally happy to chat the night away.

Speaking of adapting, in late July 2017, I started researching low carb recipes to see if that method of eating was something I could handle. My weight was climbing and getting out of control, and I was certainly starting to feel it physically. I decided to change my eating habits the first week of August and saw a difference very quickly. I managed to lose thirty-five pounds in four to five months without really trying. During this time I convinced myself that the Discovery Hearing would never take place, therefore, the sense of urgency to get ready for it had become nonexistent. Yes, again just a way for me to avoid doing something that I expected would be overwhelming.

Now over a year later I've been somewhat successful with the low carb way of eating. I've managed to lose over forty-five pounds and keep it off. I was hoping it would help me physically, but I'm still working on that solving those problems.

CHAPTER 15
THE DISCOVERY HEARING

After some back and forth between the lawyers, it was agreed upon that the Discovery Hearing would start in October. I'll share with you what it's been like since Oct 19th, 2018 when it started.

I guess I went into this thinking I would be empowered by the process. After all, it was what I had been working towards, but for me up to this point that hadn't been the case. Now maybe it would come to a close, yet at that moment I wasn't feeling that was going to happen. One good thing was that the defendant chose not to attend my deposition which he was legally entitled to do. I had expected him to be there to intimidate me, but he didn't want to hear what I had to say.

I was left a bit rattled after the first part of the Discovery. It left me feeling vulnerable and embarrassed by some of the things the defendant's lawyer questioned me on relating to medical documents and other things in my past. I was somewhat confused by the line of questioning, but remained very composed and calm during the Discovery. I was also taken off guard by having to return for more questions two weeks later as I had been under the impression it would take one day to depose me and half a day each for my sister and the plaintiff.

I started to panic the day after my first full day of questioning when it started to sink in that they had requested all my personal notes, emails and whatever else from all professionals that I'd sought help from throughout the years. I immediately lost all trust in the process and shut down. It no longer felt safe for me to talk to anyone thinking that whatever I said would have to be made available to him and his lawyer.

My lawyer somewhat reassured me by saying that any request for any of that information other than what we are comfortable providing would have to be made through the court, and every request would cost them a significant amount of money since we would also appeal the decision should these records etc. be subpoenaed. Nonetheless it was possible that we would lose the appeal for information although my lawyer didn't think a judge would allow that since it could discourage anyone in the future from seeking help knowing these types of documents could be accessed.

By this time I was feeling extremely exposed knowing that every feeling or thought that I'd expressed either in emails or in therapy could become available to him and his lawyer and subsequently would also become a permanent record of the court. I knew there was nothing there that would harm my case: if anything, it would help it, but that didn't make me feel any better. I'd battled with feeling different or as I usually say "like a freak" most of my life, and this magnified it one thousand percent. Even in the words of this book, there's still a lot of shame attached to a lot of the things I've shared.

I showed up for the second part and again more of the same questions were asked of me, mostly inquiring into my medical record relating to a pretty dark place in my life. I had been diagnosed in my early twenties as having a Borderline Personality Disorder by a psychiatrist who spent all of maybe an hour with me if that. I was never informed of that diagnosis and would only become aware of this several years later. I was diagnosed properly with PTSD a few years later by a psychologist. Both diagnoses share some of the same symptoms. The lawyer seemed to think it was important to point this out over and over again as I guess he wanted it on record. I wasn't there to defend my diagnosis. I was there only to answer "Yes... no..." or "I don't recall."

On the second round of questioning, out of the blue the other lawyer looked at me and said, "Okay. So now tell me what happened that night." I took a deep breath and started voicing for the first time ever what happened that night. I remember my voice started to crack a bit and my hands started to shake when I got to a specific part of my story. I put my head down to compose myself and at that point both lawyers called for a break. I remember rushing to the bathroom and trying to hold myself together, telling myself "You can't break now. You have to get this done." The flashbacks were so vivid and they appeared so real I could actually feel them. I wouldn't allow myself to cry because I didn't think I would be able to pull myself back together. I eventually went back in and finished the story, but I don't remember doing it. All I recall after that was my lawyer telling me on the way out that I rocked it and my first thought was I wish I had been there to see that.

Voicing my story left me feeling broken, sad, angry, afraid, ashamed, and a whole lot of other feelings I won't go into except to say that empowered wasn't one of them. It's been a battle for me since then to try and keep the flashbacks and all those feeling in a place where it feels like they're under control. I haven't been very successful at it. I knew going for acupuncture or any kind of massage would be difficult, and it was, because just the touch of another human being makes me want to curl up and disappear. It really intensifies my anxiety.

Everything was overwhelming at the time for me. I felt like I was a walking time bomb waiting to explode at any moment. I was at a place where keeping my feelings bottled in was where I preferred to be but it became increasingly more difficult for me to do. My gambling got way out of control and I know it was just another way in which to berate myself. It's like I used it to punish myself and prove that I was stupid and it confirmed all the other things that kept me feeling broken.

Was this all part of the healing process? Hell if I know, but it's where I was at that very moment.

Not knowing what was next in this process didn't help either. Being a control freak makes it very hard for me to stay grounded when I can't see what's coming. From what I knew, he would be served with another lawsuit in a few weeks. This suit was filed back in September, but the paper hadn't been served on him yet. My lawyer was hoping that it would force them to settle and, if not, then we would set dates for the rest of the Discovery. In the meantime, we'd gather the information they had requested and present arguments for the ones we wouldn't be providing, and then get dates to move it to trial where I would once again have to tell my story out loud.

I kept going to therapy and, of course, I hated everything she suggested I try. That's the rebellious me. I want to be able to snap my fingers and have everything magically solved. Didn't I at least deserve that much? After all, I had been to hell and back. I thought maybe I was feeling a bit sorry for myself combined with a lot of anger. I went through the motions, begrudgingly started a meditation that I used to do to help me breathe better, but as usual I only did it once or twice. I had very little work at this point so that tool wasn't available to me. The Universe had aligned itself to force me to stop and do what I needed to do which was to take care of me.

CHAPTER 16

AFTER THE SHOCK

After about six weeks of extreme anxiety, I started to calm down. I needed time to absorb the shock of the hearing. I fumbled through each day feeling lost and unsure. Everything had been so magnified, but was now starting to settle. I was asked at my last therapy session if I had taken the time to reflect over the events of the past year and, of course, I hadn't. I had done everything but that as I just wanted to escape it all.

By now it was December 31, 2018, and I must say that year was certainly an interesting one. Looking back it was as if everything that happened to me had been set in motion so that I could be right here, in this moment writing about it. I've used my work throughout the years as an escape from my daily life and oddly enough this year my work contracts started drying up. I was left with a lot of time on my hands which I thought was going to drive me crazy. In hindsight, I can see that it was needed to force me to do things that I normally would avoid doing.

I spent more hours outside over the summer, mowing, landscaping, and watering the gardens which had always been Denise's job. Feeding and taking care of the multiple varieties of birds and small animals that visited our backyard became a daily routine. These little things kept me grounded when everything around me felt so crazy. We created a little haven in our back yard and I've enjoyed the company of mallard ducks, a rabbit, several different finches, woodpeckers, juncos, doves, squirrels, chipmunks, a pheasant (nicknamed Charlotte), and a red cardinal. It's quite peaceful in our backyard.

The last few months of 2018 I even went for walks to try and get away from myself. It didn't really work yet it got me out of the house. I may be overly disciplined in some areas, but physical exercise is not one of them. Then I noticed I was singing again and laughing. I must say I've grown a lot in the last year and have taken major steps towards giving myself permission to be okay, all brokenness included.

I read a report provided for the trial from one of my therapists that stated "Such a traumatic ordeal is a life sentence and she will always be vulnerable to triggers of recollection and fluctuating anxiety levels." I must say I was angered when I first read that and my mission at that very moment was to prove her wrong. I understand now what she meant, and yes, it will require that I continue to work at finding ways to deal with these triggers when they happen.

I've also come to realize that the final outcome of these legal issues no longer has a hold on me. It's already given me everything that I need to continue to heal. This process gave me a VOICE and I now feel more empowered than ever. Of course, the final outcome will offer justice and a closure if it ever gets there. It will never make me whole and that is what I yearned for more than anything. I'm starting to understand that living in the moment, also referred to as mindfulness, seems to be the key. Not easy for someone like me to do. I've scoffed at this concept many times throughout the years. It sounds too simple and stupid to me. It means being with your thoughts as they are, neither grasping at them nor pushing them away. No judgement, just being.

Will it be smooth sailing from here? Surely not. Life is life with all its ups and downs. There will be challenges, but I no longer fear them. I'm not looking at climbing mountains or jumping out of planes, and I don't need to be recognized for my accomplishments. I simply want to be able to feel joy, love, and life instead of dread, fear, and darkness. I needed to come out of the shadows and into the light where my voice would be heard. Not an easy task for me. It means that I'm allowing people to see me, *all* of me, including the broken me and the vulnerable me. Something I fought and worked very hard to keep hidden for far too long.

My partner, my rock, required surgery earlier this month and it was to be a routine appendectomy. We laughed that at seventy she would need to have it removed. She had complications shortly after the surgery, but they were not related to it. She developed a major infection in a tooth causing the root to die. To watch her be in so much pain from that toothache was heart wrenching. It took a few days for the pain to subside and I saw for the first time how truly precious she was to me. I felt completely powerless. I couldn't make it better and I couldn't protect her from the pain either.

She is so important in my world and I was always afraid to allow myself to feel that for fear of what it would do to me if she was no longer there. It robbed me from many years of being in the moment with her. I feel blessed to have a chance to experience that now for however much time we have left together. Every day I feel my heart overflows with good emotions. Since I'm such an early riser, it makes me smile to hear her snore. Yes, she will probably hate to see that tidbit about her in print, but I'm sure she'll forgive me. I love how we make each other laugh first thing in the morning.

I make us breakfast every morning. You can often hear CNN on the television in the background which also offers us many laughs discussing the latest US President tweets and antics. Denise usually can be found playing Angry Birds, her favourite game, simultaneously. I often find myself humming or whistling, peaking out the window at the wildlife in the backyard to see if the red cardinal is there. Charlotte (the pheasant), will often interrupt as she makes her way in for her breakfast. This morning for the first time she came pecking at the patio door. She slowly moved back when she saw me approaching, and I gently opened the door just enough to throw a handful of sunflower seeds onto the deck. She gladly ate them all and went on her way. I make time for these things now simply because it's important and makes me feel good.

Will this peacefulness last? It can if I continue to work at it and allow it to happen. I'm sure I will have periods where I will struggle with what I call my logical side when my emotions will feel a bit overwhelming. You can't erase years of conditioning in a few months. I'm learning to trust the process and that feeling emotions can be a good thing, even if it doesn't always feel like it at the time.

This past year I've had the opportunity to spend time with my family, actual quality time, because I chose to be present. They have made several trips to come and visit with us, and I truly enjoy spending time with them. I still find it difficult to return to my hometown even for short visits. There are still many triggers there for me. Some may lessen over time and it may never be a comfortable place for me to be, but I'm okay with that now. I can respect that fact, even though I struggle a bit with it at times. I can also say today that I love my family with all their little quirks and differences. The bottom line is that they are there for me and always have been: I just wasn't able to see it.

As of the writing of this book, I'm fifty-three and still can't sleep in the dark. I struggle with a feeling of suffocating when in small enclosed places. I go to sleep every night in my bed, but still finish most of my nights on the sofa after waking up feeling like the room is closing in on me. I've learned to live with this and no longer get upset. I do on occasion get to wake up in my bed after a full night's sleep and maybe someday that will occur more often than not, but for now it's still a luxury.

The majority of the time, I've learned to integrate periods of rest into my life and if someday that improves, then I'll make the necessary changes to accommodate that. I still have control issues and, yes still need a nightlight, but have realized that I don't need everything to be perfect to be okay, I just need to embrace what makes me different. My strength, resilience, courage, determination, and at times faith come from what I used to think made me a freak.

I don't have any great words of wisdom for those of you who are struggling like me. There's no magical cure: a "one size fits all" treatment doesn't exist. All I can say is keep working at it until you get to where you need to be, and once you think you've arrived, keep working at it some more. Don't be afraid to reach out to whoever you think can help you and walk away from those who don't. I've met and worked with many people throughout my journey, both conventional and unconventional therapies, from psychologists, medical doctors, acupuncturists, naturopaths, massage therapists, hypnotherapists, psychics, mediums, shamans, healers, a social worker, and friends. Some I had more success with than others. All I want to say is try to be open to everything and they will help you get to your destination as they have for me.

What will the next year bring? Endless possibilities *if* I chose to participate and truly live in the moment. Trauma no longer needs to define who I am or who I can be. I want to start everyday laughing and be able to tell the people around me that I love them. I started a routine a few years ago that helps me achieve my morning goals of having a good chuckle. I began posting a joke on Facebook every morning. I would search the web until I found one that made me laugh and then would share it on my wall. It's became a thing and some of my friends even check in with me if I miss a day or two of posting. They look forward to it every day almost as much as I do. We laugh because now I can say I have followers – the good kind.

My job used to define me because it's all I felt I was good at. Now I simply want to be able to do a job that I love which keeps me challenged. I may not have any formal education past high school, yet I'm able to make a great living. I'm not a "girly girl": no high heels, makeup or dresses here, but I can stand tall and not be ashamed of whom I am today. I also try not to judge others. Instead I want to learn why people do what they do and what their journey has been like. I know I can make a difference in the lives of the people around me. Sometimes just asking how a person is doing and actually listening can save their life. Everything together fills that hole a little each day and makes me feel like I'm becoming what I longed to be – WHOLE.

PERSPECTIVE ONE
ELISABETH POIRIER M.A.PS, RETIRED PSYCHOLOGIST (LIC)

The following report was obtained during the gathering of evidence for the civil suit filed against my rapist.

Re: LEGERE, Nancy
    DOB:1965-04-18
    File#:117 263

The following is a response to your request for a summary of my involvement with the above named client. I first met Ms. Legere on December 11, 1990 and have seen her at different intervals until 2010. Please find included an Appendix with all the sessions she had between 1990 and 2010.

When I first met her she was 25 yrs old, single, living in Beresford and working in accounting. She had received my name through a friend whom had encouraged her to seek counseling.

During my initial assessment (sessions on December 11 and 21, 1990) the following information was gathered.

She shared that she had been sexually abused at age 8 by a male babysitter. As she was able to share her story over the course of several years, the details of the incident emerged and it became evident that she had been forced to have oral sex and raped by the said babysitter.

The reason she was now seeking therapy was that for the past 2 to 3 years it had started to become a problem in her life. She had started a relationship and had difficulties with physical contacts so was unable to continue the relationship.

Her feelings about the abuse were the following:

- She felt dirty physically – was taking at least 2 showers a day and had developed skin irritation.
- She felt empty – a void that she could not fill or know how to.
- She felt shame – she was convinced that what had happened that night was her fault because she had went to sit on the couch next to him, at his request.
- She felt hurt – and did not know how to deal with these feelings.
- She felt angry – and turned the anger towards her. Had developed a drinking problem from early teens until she was 19 yrs old. Went to AA but did not feel she would survive. She has maintained her sobriety since then. She became very active in the AA organization for several years after.

During these sessions we also identified that she had developed the following survival skills (coping mechanisms):

- Rationalizing;
- Perfectionism;
- Compulsive Washing;
- Avoiding intimacy;
- Staying in control at all cost (and even when drinking excessively);
- Staying busy;
- Alcoholism;
- Workaholism;
- Insomnia (could only sleep well during the day);
- Hypervigilance;
- Denial (maybe it didn't happen);

- Trust issues (not allowing anyone in);
- Forgetting things;
- Feeling over responsible for other people;
- Minimizing ("No big deal eh") and
- Disconnecting from feelings.

Diagnosis: (Reference from Diagnostic Criteria from DSM-IV-TR)
- <u>Post-traumatic stress disorder – PTSD</u>. Events and symptoms concurrent with this clinical diagnosis are the following:
- Experienced an event that involved an actual threat to the physical integrity of the self
- Response to such an event involve fear, helplessness, horror and physical pain
- Recurring intrusive and distressing recollections of the event with images, thoughts and perceptions
- Recurring distressing dreams of the event
- Dissociative flashback episode – reliving the traumatic event in the present as if it was recurring
- Intense psychological distress at exposure to external or internal cues that symbolize or resemble aspects of the event. (Ex: client still has to this day an acute stress response to possibly and/or seeing her alleged abuser)
- Physiological reaction (body memory) to cues that resemble or symbolize the traumatic event (ex: During flashbacks had difficulty breathing that triggered asthma attacks
- Persistent avoidance response and numbing of general responsiveness associated with the trauma. Example of this are efforts to avoid thoughts, feelings, conversations associated with trauma as well as avoiding activities, places or people that could cause recollections of the trauma
- Feelings of detachment or estrangement with others
- Restricted range of affect (Uses control to numb all her feelings, pleasant and unpleasant)
- Sense of uncertain future (Ex: does not expect to have a normal life

and not even a long life)

- Hyperarousal/Hypervigilance. Difficulty falling or staying asleep: irritability and frustrations, difficulty concentrating and exaggerated startled response

These disturbances cause clinically significant distress and/or impairment in social, occupational, or other important areas of functioning

When symptoms last more than three months the condition is considered "chronic".

SUMMARY OF INTERVENTION

From 1991 to 1993 Ms. Legere was unable to talk about the traumatic experience but she continued to come to her sessions on a regular basis. During this time therapy focused on educating and normalizing her response at the time of the event as well as the survived skills she developed to deal with the impacts of the event. Also offered were: Behavioral-cognitive techniques, Relaxation techniques, Crisis intervention and Support therapy. She was assigned tasks and was able to accomplish most.

From 1994 to 1995, she started to tell her story of the traumatic event using mostly written words. These years in therapy were very difficult for her as she had let go many of her survival skills in order to give voice to her traumatic experience. During this time therapy focused on techniques to help her "stay in the present" and manage her "Flashbacks." Also used Behavioral-cognitive therapy, Solution-focused therapy, Crisis intervention and support therapy. She continued to work on the tasks assigned during therapy. During these years of intense therapy Ms. Legere experienced gains in dealing with her trauma. However such a traumatic ordeal is a life sentence and she will always be vulnerable to triggers of recollection and fluctuating anxiety levels.

Ms. Legere was unable to continue working in a structured work environment and had to declare bankruptcy during this time. She has maintained her accounting work by starting her own business so she could work from her home. This implied working hard to establish herself in order to get enough contracts to support herself.

Ms. Legere is a very strong and independent individual which has helped her survive, function in her business, create and maintain new relationships in her professional and personal life. Over the years, she has moved to different places in New Brunswick and to Alberta for her work. She noted that her stay in Alberta was where she felt the happiest as there were almost no possibility of triggers to cause recollection of her traumatic event. Although she has learned many techniques to deal with intrusive thoughts, flashbacks and anxiety, she is now re-experiencing many of these symptoms since she decided to legally pursue the individual at this time.

Following the years of intense therapy (19914 to 1995), I continued seeing Ms. Legere at her request between 2002 to 2010 (see Appendix for dates of sessions). Most of these sessions focused on either new memories of the trauma, stressful life events at the present time, unplanned sightings of the alleged abuser when visiting family in Bathurst and triggers of recollections of her trauma. Since 2010, I have met with her informally to answer her questions or direct her to other resources. Over the last five years she has shared her traumatic experience with her parents and two sisters. With new information she now knows that the traumatic event happened when she was 7 years old.

I hope this brief summary of my lengthy involvement with this client will be helpful to you in assisting Ms. Legere. Should you have any additional questions or need further information please do not hesitate to contact me.

Yours truly,
Elisabeth Poirier M.A.Ps
(Lic) Psychologist
2015-11-18

PERSPECTIVE TWO
CONNIE BRYAR, LONGTIME FRIEND

I was introduced to Nancy some 30+ years ago at a dance. If I'm not mistaken, it might have even been at an Alcoholic Anonymous celebration dance, where she was the DJ. The boyfriend I had at that time was also an on again/off again Alcoholics Anonymous group member and knew Nancy from AA.

It's not far-fetched to think I may have also seen Nancy around the hall of Alcoholics Anonymous prior to us formally being introduced. I, myself, was just starting on my own journey of self-discovery/self-improvement in Al-Anon and periodically attended Alcoholic Anonymous open meetings to learn and support my then boyfriend who was struggling with addiction. I came to find out later that Nancy herself was a recovering alcoholic with many years of sobriety. I thought to myself "How can someone so young have so many years of sobriety?" Even back then, I was impressed at the courage she had to be able to stop drinking when people our age were usually just beginning the partying and drinking phase. It took several years from that point to realize and come to understand the torment and demons that Nancy was dealing with at that time.

From the start, I felt an instant connection with Nancy. I continued to attend open meetings with the alcoholic in my life, and would often talk to Nancy afterwards. We soon became good friends. Today I'm fortunate and grateful to refer to Nancy as my best friend and part of my extended family.

When I first met Nancy, I felt broken, full of anger and at times rage, blaming the alcoholics in my life for everything that went wrong or was going wrong in my life. I found myself often venting to Nancy. She became a regular at my house and we were soon "regulars" at Tim Hortons where we would spend several hours chatting. Well, me talking mostly, or should I say blaming others for my life's woes, while Nancy listened patiently.

Looking back at that time now and having a much better understanding of how life works and of myself, I'm positive as Nancy listened to me blame others for what was going wrong in my life all those years ago, she probably thought to herself "This poor girl hasn't got a clue what real trouble is." Nevertheless, she stuck with me and I'm so grateful and honored that we have continued to support each other throughout the years and remain great friends.

Regardless of the baggage both Nancy and I brought with us, we have had a great supportive relationship, whether it was just sitting having coffee and chatting, riding around town with the top down in her MG Midget listening to music. I might also add that she loved to make fun of me as I nursed several hangovers, and I also enjoyed driving back and forth to and from her monthly out of town therapy sessions. As hard as those therapy sessions were for Nancy, we made the best of it and supported one another through the rough patches the best way we knew how. Sometimes that meant simply sitting in silence for a while.

At some point in our friendship, Nancy felt comfortable enough to tell me of her sexual abuse, however, specific details were never discussed till years later. As inquisitive as I can be, I knew enough not to push for details in fear that it would be too upsetting for her. Instead, I just listened when she finally decided to tell me what happened. From time to time, I had enough courage to ask questions, knowing that as soon as I got "the look" from her, enough had been said and the subject was quickly changed.

It has never been easy for Nancy to talk about Nancy and she portrayed herself as "tough gal" which she was. Today I refer to her as being a strong, smart, independent woman and who has much to offer to anyone and everyone. I was aware enough back then to see through the façade and walls she had built around herself which, in my opinion, were necessary for her own protection and survival.

Although I moved away from our hometown some 23+ years ago, we've made efforts to remain in contact and in each other's lives. Throughout the years, I've seen Nancy grow tremendously. First finding Denise, the love of her life, to 30+ years later continuing to push forward on her life-long journey to find peace and contentment within herself. Many would have given up the fight! Today, she even lets me hug her when we do see one another and hugs back which is a huge accomplishment. She laughs and there's calmness about her. Her growth is obvious as there's a visible lightness about her and I can see that she feels more comfortable in her own skin and strives to stay that way.

Nancy has not allowed her past to get the best of her, nor to define her. In having multiple (we try to meet up at least every second month) conversations with her the past few years, I've recognized that she's become more comfortable talking in detail about her sexual abuse, thus making me more aware and have better insight as to what she's had to deal with and continues to overcome in her life. Still after 46 years since the sexual abuse, Nancy continues to push through the aftermath of sexual abuse with her reoccurring anxiety attacks (or whatever medical term that is) from time to time. The only difference is that now she quickly finds a means of support to help her through the tough days/nights. Make no mistake, I don't mean dealing by gambling. (I had to throw that in.)

I could not be prouder of the progress she's made throughout the years and the fact that she found enough strength and courage to not give up on herself and the world (which I'm sure she thinks might have been easier at times), to sitting down and writing an actual book about her life, the sexual abuse, and the impacts and aftermath caused by the sexual abuse.

As I think of Nancy today, I get goosebumps and my heart is filled with astonishment, pride, and love as she continues the fight for the life I think she finally recognizes she deserves. I'm floored by her perseverance and the hard work she puts into addressing or dealing with the memories of her past as they continue to come back and try to bite her in the ass.

I am so **very grateful** for the lifelong friendship we've cultivated and so **very proud** of you for everything you've accomplished and the efforts you go through to become the best version of yourself possible. I love you Nancy!

PERSPECTIVE THREE
DAWN MCKELVIE CYR, MA

PERSPECTIVE ON CHILDHOOD SEXUAL ABUSE: DISCOVERY, TREATMENT, AND HEALING

DAWN MCKELVIE CYR, MA

When Nancy asked me if I wanted to add my perspective about her journey with PTSD, addiction, and childhood sexual abuse to her book, I was immediately on board. Any book that shines a light on the subject of childhood sexual abuse and its effects on the survivor is enormously important. It's a subject that usually stays locked away in a closet or the dark recesses of a person's memory forever. Some have an inkling – some distant wisp of a scattered memory or a flash of a snapshot, but are afraid to visit it for fear they might be making it up because the pictures aren't clear. Then there are those who know exactly what has happened to them, but have never told anyone because of shame and guilt. Others have a recollection of the abuse, but minimize the impact it has had in their lives because it happened so long ago. *"I've dealt with it and it wasn't that bad"* are words I often hear when or if they talk about it at all.

I have seen all of these scenarios in the women I have worked with who have been abused. Yet what's remarkable is that they rarely come to therapy with the conscious understanding that what is at the root of their struggles is the abuse. They come in because they're feeling depressed, anxious, angry, or lost; some aren't feeling much at all, they're just numb. They're may be having difficulties in their relationships or in their work. They usually suffer from low self-esteem, and may have issues with alcohol or drugs or food. They might be self-harming or have a history of eating disorders. They have somatic or physical symptoms such as migraines, IBS, and insomnia. Many have a history of unstable interpersonal relationships and dissociative episodes. Some have received a diagnosis around depression and anxiety, avoidant or borderline personality disorder. They know the list of symptoms and diagnoses off by heart. But what they often don't know, but desperately want to know is the why. Why do they have such a complex list? And why can't they seem to get better?

As I take into account these symptoms and their story begins to unfold in our sessions, it becomes clear that something traumatic has happened to them. These are many of the symptoms of Post-traumatic stress disorder, or PTSD, and though it is not a recognized diagnosis in the Diagnostic and Statistical Manual of Mental Disorders, version 5, (DSM-5), more specifically complex Post-traumatic stress disorder (C-PTSD). That's when I ask the question, one that so often does not get asked outright: do you recall ever having been sexually abused as a child? I believe as therapists we need to make this question a part of our intake forms and then we need to ask it out loud. In my experience, the when of asking depends on timing and only after I believe we have established a strong therapeutic alliance with our client. They have to be able to trust us in order to be able to share something so horrible and painful as this. This is when I connect the dots and where I help them begin to see all the past diagnoses not as independent issues, but as symptoms of *the* issue: the childhood sexual abuse. This is where the real work begins.

Different therapists practice different forms of therapy. The most important thing to remember is that no single therapy or technique holds all of the answers for healing. Again, I believe first and foremost the therapeutic relationship is key to helping a client move through the deeply personal and often painful journey of healing from childhood sexual abuse. If you don't trust your therapist, you cannot share and be open about some of the most painful and difficult moments you have experienced. From there I believe multiple approaches combined with education are the best practices. What does this client need at this moment in their recovery: psychodynamic talk therapy, cognitive behaviour, solution focused, narrative, etc. What does the client respond to in this moment? Whatever the specific therapy might be, I do believe that it should be provided within a phased framework; a process used by many trauma therapists and researchers. Very basically it is outlined as follows:

Phase one deals mainly with psychoeducation for the patient about a) short and long-term effects of trauma; b) safety – in the therapeutic relationship, in the home, in the outside environment; and c) stability – with eating, sleeping, and the ability to care for and soothe themselves;

Phase two deals mainly with traumatic memories and experiences – how to process and integrate the negative aspects such as grief and Post-traumatic symptoms, and how to create newer positive and desensitized models;

Phase three deals with coming back into the here and now.

An important point to remember is that there is movement between the phases. And that is just fine. As a new memory comes to the surface, the therapist might have to move back to the safety phase before moving forward. It will be different for every client as each of them have their own story to tell and their own journey to healing. Just as Nancy had hers and so bravely shared in this book. It often takes years to get to the point where Nancy is today, so be patient and kind to yourself. Don't be rushed. This is your story to tell, your journey to take, your road to understanding, healing, and finally, recovery. Tell it in your voice in whatever way you find that works for you. Whatever way you chose to use, I wholeheartedly encourage you to tell it, because there *can* be healing and you are worthy of receiving it.

Made in the USA
Columbia, SC
13 April 2019